Spoon Fed

Spoon Fed

HOW EIGHT COOKS
SAVED MY LIFE

KIM SEVERSON

Riverhead Books
a member of Penguin Group (USA) Inc.
New York
2010

RIVERHEAD BOOKS
Published by the Penguin Group
Penguin Group (USA) Inc., 375 Hudson Street, New York,
New York 10014, USA • Penguin Group (Canada), 90 Eglinton Avenue East,
Suite 700, Toronto, Ontario M4P 2Y3, Canada (a division of Pearson
Penguin Canada Inc.) • Penguin Books Ltd, 80 Strand, London WC2R 0RL,
England • Penguin Ireland, 25 St Stephen's Green, Dublin 2, Ireland
(a division of Penguin Books Ltd) • Penguin Group (Australia),
250 Camberwell Road, Camberwell, Victoria 3124, Australia (a division of
Pearson Australia Group Pty Ltd) • Penguin Books India Pvt Ltd,
11 Community Centre, Panchsheel Park, New Delhi–110 017, India •
Penguin Group (NZ), 67 Apollo Drive, Rosedale, North Shore 0632,
New Zealand (a division of Pearson New Zealand Ltd) • Penguin Books
(South Africa) (Pty) Ltd, 24 Sturdee Avenue, Rosebank,
Johannesburg 2196, South Africa

Penguin Books Ltd, Registered Offices:
80 Strand, London WC2R 0RL, England

Portions of chapters five, eight, and nine appeared,
in slightly different form, in *The New York Times.*

Library of Congress Cataloging-in-Publication Data

Severson, Kim.
Spoon fed : how eight cooks saved my life / Kim Severson.
p.   cm.
ISBN 978-1-59448-757-6
1. Cookery.   2. Cooks.   3. Severson, Kim.   I. Title.
TX652.S476   2010   2009041038
641.5—dc22

Printed in the United States of America
1   3   5   7   9   10   8   6   4   2

BOOK DESIGN BY AMANDA DEWEY

The publisher is not responsible for your specific health or allergy needs that may require medical
supervision. The publisher is not responsible for any adverse reactions to the recipes contained
in this book.

While the author has made every effort to provide accurate telephone numbers and Internet
addresses at the time of publication, neither the publisher nor the author assumes any
responsibility for errors, or for changes that occur after publication. Further, the publisher does
not have any control over and does not assume any responsibility for author or third-party websites
or their content.

*Penguin is committed to publishing works of quality and integrity.
In that spirit, we are proud to offer this book to our readers;
however, the story, the experiences, and the words
are the author's alone.*

For Katia and Sammy

Spoon Fed

Introduction

For much of my young life, I ate my meals at a big oak kitchen table that my dad, in a mash-up of fashion and thrift, had painted black. That was before I was born, when black and white were in vogue and the Severson family was just getting started. The other table in the house, the fancy one in the dining room, was reserved for Christmas dinners and birthday parties and visits from relatives. But even before I was old enough to carry my empty cereal bowl to the sink, I knew the real action was at that black kitchen table.

Over a million meals there, our lives played out in front of one another. We five Severson kids—Keith, Kent, Kim, Keely and Kris—took instruction on how to become good citizens and helpful guests. We learned to be part of a tribe. And we figured out how to behave. Making my sister, Keely, laugh so hard that milk poured from her nose wasn't cool. Bringing home a good report card was.

Depending on the day, I arrived at the dinner table happy, sad, angry or bored. As a teenager, I sometimes showed up stoned. I once sat at that table for hours, refusing to eat green beans despite my father's declaration that my freedom could be earned with just three bites. But mostly, our meals did not include much drama. I lived a middle-class childhood of pork chops, baked potatoes and milk, punctuated with bursts of ambitious cooking for dinner parties and holidays.

My rock-solid dad, James Howard Severson, fought the good fight in the middle management battlefield of a national tire company. He comes from Norwegian stock. Although he likes a good martini and prefers the woods to all other places, he was never a man prone to playing hooky or calling in sick, even if he was. "Just don't be a burden on society," he'd say when we came to him for advice on what to do with our lives. Every morning he would wipe a bit of fried egg from his fingers, scoot back a chair and head out the door with his briefcase. The goal was to leave the office early enough to make it to one of the ball games or music recitals or swim meets that rolled through our lives in an endless loop.

By the time he left in the morning, my mom, Anne Marie Severson, had already been at work for hours. Her people were Italian, and the kitchen was her office. Brown paper lunch sacks had to be filled with apples and sandwiches. A Bundt cake had to be baked for a volunteer group luncheon. Something had to become dinner. She had been a farm girl whose childhood home in the far north Wisconsin woods saw its first refrigerator when she was in elementary school. As a result, she embraced every new twist of kitchen technology. We had a crepe pan and a food processor before anyone else on the block, and she prized her rectangular harvest gold electric frying pan. She ran the kind of efficient and reliable home kitchen that's hard to find these days.

On the surface, I looked like a lot of other resilient, freckled kids. I was athletic and social. But I was the middle child, pulled by the moods of the siblings above and below me. And I was eager to make myself an integral part of household business. (Others might say, less politely, that I was nosy.) I was desperate to stand out in a family that prized the team, but I was more sensitive than I let on. I felt overwhelmed by the world, and my solution was a constant quest to fit into it somehow. This was exhausting. At the end of the day, arriving home to that kitchen brought instant relief. I relied on my mom's predictable roster of lasagna and fried chicken and even the dry venison roasts from deer my dad had shot. And I especially loved it when she would get fired up on a mix of women's magazines and boredom and we would eat with a certain middle-class culinary panache. Pasta alla carbonara, Oriental pepper steak and French crepes would appear like exotic relatives.

Despite the warmth and consistency that came from that kitchen, pity the child who pushed things too far. Who can forget the afternoon my oldest brother, Keith, smarted off one too many times? My mother hit him in the head with a frozen bass. That night, the bass was on the table. To this day, he still doesn't care much for fish. Still, no matter what happened during the day, no matter how many times you took a frozen fish to the head, getting back to that table by dinner was the one rule you absolutely wanted to obey—at least, it was the one I tried to obey even when I became a teenager and discovered how many rules there were to break. The table was where I was safe. It was home. And when my mother started to teach her earnest little elementary school daughter to put dinner on that table, she gave me everything I needed to know to make a safe home when I grew up.

The problem is, somewhere between those early lessons and the ones I am trying to teach my own young daughter, I stumbled hard and lost my way. It would take a series of women who knew how to cook to reteach me the life lessons I forgot and to teach me the ones I never learned in the first place. Most of those lessons—simple truths about the way life works—have been delivered in complex wrappers that have taken me years to open. Others were hidden in the smallest of packages delivered by the most unexpected people.

Let me give you a little example. Early one cold California morning, long after I had started my career as a newspaper reporter, I stumbled out of my car chilled and stiff. I had driven for an hour northwest from Berkeley to Inverness, a tiny town near the Point Reyes National Seashore. My editor at the *San Francisco Chronicle* wanted me to write about Margaret Grade, a psychiatrist who runs a quirky little inn that was popular with chefs and actors. They liked the peace and quiet of her down-covered beds and her quirky affection for taxidermy and old books. They had also fallen for the food she made from local eggs, fish and vegetables that people with names like Eat Dog and Lumpy delivered to her doorstep.

I walked around to the back of the inn until I found a heavy wooden door. I pushed hard against it and took a few tentative steps into a dark kitchen. Before I could even unbutton my coat and say hello, Margaret appeared out of nowhere and slipped a spoonful of warm polenta in my mouth. She had been up for a couple of hours already, kayaking in from her house across the water. She had put some scones in the oven and then got busy melting Taleggio into soft cornmeal. To finish her porridge, she stirred in pieces of meaty chanterelle mushrooms that had pushed themselves up in nearby woods only a couple of days earlier.

The warmth of the cornmeal hit me first, wiping away the chill. Then came the tang of the cheese, working like a bright, creamy tonic on my sleepy senses. The mushrooms offered a solid sense of place and closed the deal. In the moment it took to pass the spoon from her pot to my mouth, we bonded. Two strangers became friends. We were women who were willing to stop whatever we were doing and stand in awe of something good to eat. I left at the end of that day with a nice newspaper story, but I also had a little life lesson in my back pocket: Giving someone a taste of something delicious at exactly the right moment is a fail-safe way to start a good relationship.

I have made it this far in life only because people took the time to teach me those kinds of lessons. And the biggest lessons were delivered in the kitchen, given to me by women who made their families dinner every night, who saved favorite recipes to pass on and needed only a paring knife and a sturdy spoon.

I'm one of those people who grew up in the backwash of the Baby Boom. We are a generation of adults who didn't get our first computers until college and now live in a world defined by Google searches, video clips and smart phones we will never really figure out. My generation wasn't issued a GPS device, and the previous generation didn't leave us directions. Certainly not directions to the kitchen. The kitchen was a prison for the wave of feminists that included Hillary Clinton and her Wellesley sisters. When Hillary's husband was running for president the first time, she said, "I suppose I could have stayed home and baked cookies and had teas, but what I decided to do was fulfill my profession." The editors at *Family Circle* magazine, in a rare moment of genius that had both political junkies and home bakers applauding, decided to stage a bake-off: Hillary Clinton v. Barbara Bush. Contender v. Incumbent. One Round. One Recipe.

When the dust settled, Hillary's way with chocolate chip cookie dough carried the day. The thing that bothered me most about the cookie incident wasn't the inherent sexism. It was that Hillary acted like giving out a good cookie recipe diminished her. One can understand the insult, of course. Women still get the short end of things. When the roles were reversed and Hillary was running for president, no one asked Bill for his favorite shortbread recipe.

On the other hand, I can always use another good cookie recipe. And I want a leader who is thoughtful about these kinds of things. Having mastery of the art of cookie baking should not make one less of a person. It has, on several occasions, made me the most popular person in the room. But I didn't always see it that way. I had to learn that food is power. And it took spending time with women who don't know Twitter but understand a lot about life and cooking to teach me.

My heroes are women who never abandoned the kitchen. They use cooking as a source of strength. Their recipes have helped save their communities and kept families together. They have made political change through their love of food. These are women who can whip egg whites just long enough that they don't cross the subtle line between soft peaks and stiff. To them, braising a piece of inexpensive beef until it becomes a slick, tender miracle or picking exactly the right plum from the produce bin is as natural as turning over in bed. They also know that the best thing to do in a crisis is feed people something soothing—a cup of tea, a spoonful of warm polenta and mushrooms, a perfect roasted chicken stuffed with Meyer lemons.

I learned to cook from a series of women that begins with my mother and spills out over a decade of writing about food. My time with them, whether as brief as a handshake or as long as my life, helped me figure out how to walk through the world. Through them, I came to see that the one constant in my life, the thing that I have always been able to count on, was my ability to go to the kitchen, turn on the stove and feed someone.

The women in this book shined the light on what was ahead for me when I couldn't find my way. They showed me that food is the best antidote for anything life throws at you. They became my tour guides, helping me figure out what I really believed in, how to re-make my life and re-create a family, and, finally, how to face death.

Your life lessons might look a little different from mine. The cadence of everyone's childhood and coming of age is unique. But I venture that we could sit down at a kitchen table and find that parts of our paths look just the same. Like me, you learned from people who navigated life before you and then took the time to tell you how they did it. For me, those guides were these women. And their kitchens were my classrooms.

1

Moose Meat and Raised Waffles

D riving in the Bay Area is an art, and on a spring morning a dozen years ago it was abundantly clear that I hadn't mastered it. Not only to me, but to the people in the cars behind me.

I had pushed the gas pedal down as far as I could, willing four cylinders to cough their way up a hill and head east out of San Francisco. I could almost smell the cologne on the guy in a tie and mirrored Oakleys who shot around me in his black Honda Accord, a car I am sure he chose because he thought it combined sexy and practical in one energy-efficient package. Awesome!

My own awesome rig was a Daihatsu Rocky, white with a big French kiss of rust. It was neither sexy nor practical. Seven years earlier, when I drove the Rocky off a new car lot in Seattle and pointed it toward Alaska, I had somehow convinced myself that it was a little bit of each. I picked it because it was the only new vehicle with four-wheel drive that I could afford. I had never bought a new car before and I was close to broke. But at the time I was about to spend ten days making my way north along the Alaska-Canada Highway to my new life writing for the *Anchorage Daily News*. The thought of doing the trip in a used car made me nervous.

The truck had an overgrown black metal grill and teal detail paint that looked like big Nike swoops on the doors. Despite this, I thought it was tough in a cool-girl sort of way. Who cared if Daihatsu was a make no one had ever heard of, or that it would fade from the American market just as sections of the engine began to fail and I needed parts? It was a new truckette and it was all mine (and the bank's). Later, in one of those moments when people think their honesty about something you spent thousands of dollars on is somehow helpful, a tough boat captain friend who made her living running salmon charters out of Seward, Alaska, laughed at it.

"What you've got there," she said, "is a Barbie SUV."

Which, I thought at the time, must make me Barbie's rough-hewn little sister, the one everyone says got the personality.

The idea that I was in any way related to something Barbiesque was problematic on so many levels. First, I was never a Barbie girl. My doll of choice was the much less fashion-dependent Jane West. She had a plastic horse and a faux-leather vest. Although the ads did point out that she came with a makeup kit, which kept nervous parents from thinking Jane was too much of a tomboy, she also had a bad-ass six-shooter and rifle. In the extended imaginary games of ranch I played with my sister, Jane West did not go shopping with her doll friends. She rode her horse on the cliff that was the back of the couch and built fences alone on the living-room floor that served as my prairie. Although I was a kid at the time, I can see now why it was so easy for me to imagine that Johnny West, her Ken-like counterpart, was her brother and not her cowboy beau. It wouldn't take many months into my adolescence to figure out that I preferred to date cowgirls.

Living in a world that happily made plenty of room for Barbie posed other challenges, not just to girls like me but, it turns out, even for the girls who looked like Barbie and dated fellows who looked like Ken. I'll admit that the idea of being adored for nothing but my face and my body has had an occasional appeal, in the way winning the lottery does. The difference is that I have a much better chance of winning the lottery.

Still, my little Barbie SUV had gotten me to Alaska and back, and I was counting on it to help me navigate a new, very different place. I was in the Bay Area now, where there were more traffic lights in one of its small cities than in the whole of Alaska. Still, San Francisco was just one more new place, wrapped in all the fear and promise that had clung to every other fresh start I had made in my life.

This is the way it has been since I was a kid. My parents were dutiful players in the great corporate migration of the 1960s and '70s. My dad worked for the Uniroyal Tire Company and his rise through the ranks of mid-level management was marked with a series of moves, which were always euphemistically presented to the children as "transfers." Clearly I am someone who knows my way around a moving van. And my well-honed ability to assemble a set of grocery store cartons and fill them with the junk I called my possessions served me well when I started writing for newspapers. The digital world is changing the game fast, but in the 1980s those of us who got into journalism knew it would mean traveling from small paper to small paper like third-string circus performers until, maybe, we hit the big time.

The ability to pick up and move also turned out to be useful when life in one town started to unravel. It's not like I was trying to avoid jail or violent lovers. But when you drink hard and screw up relationships like I did, moving is a balm. The phrase tossed out in self-help groups, I believe, is "doing a geographic." But the move to California was different. The stakes were much higher. I was in San Francisco, the biggest city I had ever worked in. And I had what I thought was my dream job—writing about food for a big daily newspaper. I felt like a rookie getting called to the majors.

That's how I ended up panicked on a freeway, maneuvering my Barbie SUV through five lanes of traffic to get to Marion Cunningham's house on time.

"She's really the last great American home cook," my new boss, Michael Bauer, told me just before sending me off on one of my first assignments.

I had worked for Michael only a few months, but it was long enough to understand a few things about him. For one, I knew he loved being the executive food and wine editor of the *San Francisco Chronicle*. And he was great at it. But he could be a maddening boss. He was a compact, impeccably dressed bundle of perfection wrapped around a crystal-clear palate and a soft, soft heart. Michael could infuriate the staff to the point of mutiny one day, and the next commit such an understated, well-timed act of kindness that all was forgiven.

I knew, too, that he loved Marion Cunningham. For years, she had been his mother figure and dear friend. She was a fixture at the chummy holiday parties Michael orchestrated at his Barbara Barry-perfect home on Potrero Hill in San Francisco. She also served as a trusted companion when he was reviewing restaurants. When he took her out, chefs were so moved by her grandmotherly warmth and her reputation that they would come from the kitchen to say hello.

"They'd almost genuflect," he told me.

Michael was forever a loyal son. When Marion's dog died, he was the one who raced east from San Francisco for days in a row, tripping through shelters to find her a perfect replacement. And later, when she got too sick to manage, Michael waged a battle with her daughter over her care.

What Michael didn't know about me when he made me the newest member of his staff was that I was fighting my own battle. Three months before I moved from Alaska to work for him, I put down the bottle. This was the great cosmic joke of my life. A major newspaper offered me a job writing about food in one of the world's great wine regions just about the time I figured out that my long, deep and destructive love affair with alcohol and drugs was about to kill me.

When you get sober, everyone tells you not to make any big changes in the first year. No major geographic relocations, no quitting your job, no changes in your relationship. I had done two out of three, and the third wasn't far behind.

It would be easy to blame Alaska's six dark, grueling months of winter for accelerating my drinking, a pastime I had pursued with great enthusiasm since high school. Alaska is a place of deep extremes, and that makes it easy to drink. At a bar after work, looking for a way to kill time, someone might call out "six pack!" and the bartender would put six drinks down in front of everyone in the group. That's one bar, six drinks and fourteen hours until the sun came up again. The math made sense at the time, especially to someone who had spent most of her life drinking. I remember stealing what I could from my parents' liquor cabinet and sneaking it into the junior high school cafeteria. I had dared a kid named Doris to do it, too. She and I poured our little Tupperware containers of brown liquor into slushies we bought from the vending machine. We shared it with friends. I was instantly buzzed and instantly popular. Nirvana.

I was an addict from the start, and I still trend that way even though these days I try to limit it to work and, to a lesser degree, sugar. It's hard to explain what that feels like. I'm past thinking it comes down to willpower. For me, it's about emotional health and brain chemistry. Anyone who has found it hard to stop pouring huge amounts of liquor into their bodies but then discovered a way to navigate life without its most popular social lubricant will tell you this: Drinking too much, even when you want to stop, happens because certain people's brains are hard-wired in a mysterious, inexplicable way. You think to yourself, "If one drink feels really good and two feels really, really good, a hundred ought to feel fantastic." As sane people know, it doesn't work that way. A hundred drinks feels terrible. Bad things happen. But the addict keeps at it, thinking that at some point it's going to get good again. Gambling, stuffing your closet, serial bad lovers, pints of ice cream consumed at one sitting. It's all the same. The point is to not feel what you're feeling.

The problem is, you become someone you never thought you would become, and you have no idea how you got there. Imagining that an alcoholic will stop through sheer willpower is like believing the tumor will go away if you just wish really, really hard.

My drinking had started to feel bad more often than it felt good a couple of years before I met Michael and we started talking about a job. One of the worst side effects was that alcohol had become more important than food. That alone should have convinced me there was a problem. Food was the thing I loved, the thing that gave me confidence and solace, the thing that held my interest above all else. Where there was good food there were usually good people. I learned that early on. I also learned that making food for other people was something I was good at. It gave me a sense of peace and belonging. When I made food, I made a tribe.

In Anchorage, where we really didn't have a lot to do in the winter at night, dinner parties became a central focus of my social life. But increasingly, I had spent more time and money finding a good pinot noir than an interesting recipe for a roasted fillet of salmon with blackberries to pair it with. My focus wasn't on the first few important bites one might offer a guest before dinner, but rather on finding just the right domestic sparkler that I would pour into flutes and effortlessly hand to the guests as they walked in the door. I cringe when I look back and realize that my reasonably decent cooking skills faded after a few glasses of wine, which I drank before my guests had even started to get ready to come over. I once got my hands on a whole lobe of foie gras. Overconfident and drunk, I vaguely remember sliding pale slices of barely warm liver onto the plates of my hostages. I mean my dinner guests.

There were wine tastings where I'd start the evening by keeping careful notes, rejecting bottles with quiet arrogance and commenting on the best of the lot with what I felt was brilliant and original insight. By the end of the night, my notebook would have fallen into the toilet and the few other drunks left at the party would help me polish off the bottles we had hours earlier declared swill. Then someone would call their drug dealer.

Do this or some version of it enough times and you either die or get sober. I didn't want to die. I don't know how else to say this, because it sounds really dramatic, but the truth is I would have died if I had kept on. Not a lot of people knew how addicted I really was, how much mood altering I needed every day just to function. Let me just say, for the record, it was bad.

One day, desperate but with enough sense left to know I was about to slip completely under, I called a friend. To this day, I don't know why I picked that moment. It's the kind of thing that makes you believe that something else, something bigger, might be going on here. It's the kind of thing that makes you believe in God.

The woman I called was a lawyer who loved food and wine as much as I did. The difference was, she hadn't had a drink in twelve years and she wasn't thousands of dollars in debt, hanging on by a thread at work and thinking about suicide. I drove my little Barbie truck to her house, a triple-story mammoth in a suburb in the south end of the city. We sat on her couch and I presented my tattered case. Her ruling was simple.

"You never have to have another drink," she said, "and you need to go into treatment."

A reasonable person would have said, "Thank you very much. I wish I had thought of that myself. I'll get right to it!"

The brain of a drunk doesn't work that way. I got mad at her. She clearly hadn't understood how unique my case was. I explained how my career as a food writer, which just seemed to be getting off the ground, would be over if I couldn't drink. I bargained, confident I could find a way to control it. Maybe if I just stopped the drugs? I sobbed. I blamed Alaska. I blamed ex-lovers. At that point, I would have blamed her couch.

"It would be impossible for me to change my career," I moaned. "I need to drink to work. What the hell am I going to do?"

She told me a couple of stories. They involved lost weekends with boxes of wine in the apartments of men whose names she couldn't recall and dancing in her bra at a remote Alaska bar to celebrate a good day at work. One in particular gave me a strange sort of hope. She was at a fancy dinner when someone put a rare bottle of Lafite Rothschild on the table.

"I had to drink it," she said. "It was a work of art."

It wasn't so pretty when she threw it up later that night.

At that moment, I realized she understood how I drank, and the way my delusional mind worked. I also started to understand the dangerous illusions inherent in the food and wine business. When you're in it, it seems that everyone else can drink without consequence. So you start to believe you can. And while wine is a great thing if you don't abuse it, people will have you believe that any meal without it is somehow diminished. It turns out that a lot of people in the food and wine business do have consequences from their drinking, and that food is really quite lovely all on its own.

She handed me an address and I drove there right away. I found a roomful of people who had quit drinking. Most of them were very different from me, but we could compare notes nonetheless. My lawyer friend also told me to find out if my job would help pay for any kind of rehab. It would. And she told me to keep calling her. For reasons I will never understand, it worked. I went to rehab classes at night and I joined a therapy group. I came to see that no matter how pretty a glass of wine might seem, it was a luxury I could never again afford.

So far, I haven't had another drink.

Michael knew none of this when he hired me. In fact, I was fairly toasted during one of the dinners we had when I spent a week at the *Chronicle* trying out for the job. I'm not sure he knew, or at least he never let on. But let's just say Michael took a big risk when he hired me. It's not that I wasn't a good worker and a fast writer. Thanks to my family, I had always been an enthusiastic eater—a good fork, as the Italians say. I had been in the kitchen early, tackling cooking tasks with the same confidence other girls tackled the monkey bars.

My formal culinary education included the high school summer I helped out in the gourmet kitchen store where my mother worked for a time, putting little price tags on paring knives and stacking boxes of the wildly popular new machines called Cuisinarts. And almost every night during high school, after I got home from whatever sport I was playing, I would rush into the kitchen to help her make dinner.

But my training started much earlier, while I was still in elementary school. One of the first jobs I was handed was setting the table, a task I tried to infuse with my own budding brand of flair by folding the cheap, square paper napkins into mounds that I thought looked vaguely like pyramids, or maybe swans. Soon, I had graduated to salad making, a task that took specialized training that you could only get by enduring the wrath of the chef.

"Stop it," my mother would yell, looking over as I earnestly flailed at a head of iceberg. "You are killing that lettuce."

Lesson one: Don't stack together as many leaves as you can and then tear them like a muscle man showing off with a phone book.

"Are you trying to drown that salad?"

Lesson two: Never just pour the oil straight out of the bottle onto the vegetables unless you've got a steady hand.

"That salt is not going to put itself in there."

Lesson three: Always season the salad.

This is how I learned to cook.

One fall evening, before I was even in high school, my early training was put to the test. I was a brave, overachieving young Girl Scout with my focus fixed like a laser on securing the highly coveted cooking badge. And that would mean cooking for my family. Game on.

Every family has its code, the thing to follow that buys you a place at the table. In our family, there were a couple of things. One was our love of trophies and the other was food. We were raised to never be afraid of a competition. My dad had been a nationally ranked ski jumper and later an Olympic judge. My little brother, Kris, took up the sport. He was an ace skier who came this close to making the Olympic team. The seeds of ambition had been planted early.

I was a physical kid, which seemed to invite a certain style of physical education. Dad taught me to swim before I even hit kindergarten by holding my arm and dunking me in a pool. When it came time to learn how to water ski, I couldn't get back in the boat until I managed to stand up on the skis. My mother attended a thousand games of softball and volleyball and basketball. I can still see her on the bleachers, her purse under her arm. All of us camped and played baseball and won sack races to the best of our abilities. The results, whether a small sportsmanship ribbon from the neighborhood swim club or my brother's national championship skiing trophies, went on a set of basement shelves that became a de facto trophy case.

Still—and this remains a point of great debate (and therapy sessions, I'm sure) among my siblings—I recall that it didn't matter if you won. You just had to show up and do your best. Of course, winning was preferable, but it was more important to participate and finish what you started.

So when it came time to get that Girl Scout badge, it seemed a natural thing to mix cooking and competition, two areas around which my family orbited. Back then, Girl Scout badges were straight-forward: photography, hiking, citizenship, cooking. (Today they have gotten much more complex. To nail the Food Power badge, for example, a Girl Scout has to complete six of ten tasks. Among them is daunting task number eight: "End Hunger." I can only hope someone someday develops a real food badge, one that requires pork tastings, butchering a chicken and creating a perfect Italian meringue.)

The rules stated that I had to cook an entire meal for my family. I chose a menu based on my favorite combination at the time, and one I still like on certain nights when life hasn't tipped in my favor: fried chicken, kernels of corn and mashed potatoes. The fateful evening, I dutifully slipped on my apron and got to work, but it wasn't as easy as I'd thought. Shaking the chicken in a paper bag of flour, I somehow overlooked a hole in the bottom; the actual frying of the chicken had to be done by my mother, who seemed to believe I might set the kitchen on fire; and the mashed potatoes suffered from lumps even though I tried to approximate my mother's hip-shaking mashing method. But the frozen corn was a comparative breeze. As I carried each bowl and platter to the black wooden table, sweaty and tired and dusted in flour, I felt a perfect mix of relief and happiness. My family was eating my food, and the Girl Scout cooking badge was mine.

By college, I was frying eggs as a short-order breakfast cook and I had acquired enough skill to run a shift at the Little Caesar's pizza chain in Lansing, Michigan. I could wait tables, too. But to convince Michael to hire me, a Girl Scout badge and a waitress gig weren't going to be much help. My only professional experience writing about food had been doing a few immature reviews for my college paper, a handful of freelance stories and a steady stream of restaurant criticism in Anchorage. The town, with some 300,000 people, was not considered a nexus of culinary and journalistic greatness, though it was better than you might think on both counts.

Before Alaska, my journalism career highlights centered on hard news. I was all about digging for scandal in the local suburban school district I was assigned to cover, or writing terse paragraphs about police action in Tacoma. I eventually started to cover the growing battle between the Crips and the Bloods in Tacoma, and then sent dispatches from the bleak halls of Washington State's mental hospitals. I even interviewed serial killer Ted Bundy's mother on the eve of her son's execution in 1989. She was from Tacoma, and I worked for the local paper, the *News Tribune*. Two images stand out from the day I visited his childhood home: the huge pile of condolence cards covering a table in the living room and the Boy Scout uniform still hanging in a closet.

I was quite happy to leave the Tacoma paper and head north to work for the largest newspaper in Alaska. I was hired to write news features with an emphasis on social issues, but soon talked my way into writing about restaurants. Being the restaurant critic in Anchorage is not unlike being the best ballerina in Lubbock, Texas. I never did develop a taste for the fat and whale skin delicacy called muktuk in Yupik, but I did learn to catch salmon and had a freezer so full of pristine fillets of sockeye and coho that I brought it to potlucks or gave it away as often as I could. (Salmon is like the zucchini of Alaska.) I also picked up just enough about newspapering and food that the California editors decided to take a chance on me.

On the day I climbed into my little Rocky and headed out of the *Chronicle* offices on Mission Street to meet the famous Marion Cunningham at her house in the suburbs of Walnut Creek, I was absolutely convinced there was no way I had the tools to actually do the job they had hired me for. I knew I was headed for failure.

Now, I know interviewing an elderly woman about cooking isn't exactly grilling a corrupt corporate executive or exposing a philandering mayor, but for me it was a big assignment. I prepared like I was about to take down Nixon. I read through her half-dozen cookbooks and went to the computer archives to scan a decade's worth of her *Chronicle* cooking columns. Marion had originally made her name in the culinary world by helping James Beard with matters both professional and personal in the latter half of his outsized life as the majordomo of American cookery. They were both a breed you don't really find anymore in the food world—bona fide home cooks whose power came from writing actual cookbooks, not starring in television shows. Through him, she got a job rewriting the Fannie Farmer cookbook for Judith Jones, the tiny, focused New York book editor behind Julia Child's *Mastering the Art of French Cooking.*

But Marion's most important role might have been her years as the mother-confessor for a whole segment of the food world. Most of the notable names in the American food revolution that started in the 1970s all claimed a piece of her. It was Marion who dragged James Beard into Chez Panisse and introduced him to Alice Waters. At the time, Alice had not become the steely coquette who would revolutionize America's attitude toward seasonal organic food. She was a scared perfectionist who knew absolutely nothing about running a restaurant. Her love life was chaotic and her administrative skills questionable. But James Beard loved the place and told his national audience, essentially saving Chez Panisse from what seemed like certain bankruptcy.

A writer for *Alimentum*, a very interesting little food literature collection, interviewed Ruth Reichl about Marion a few years back.

"If you wanted to know what was going on, you called Marion," Ruth told the writer. "She was sort of a connecting force. She was very important to me, and I think she represents a fascinating story about American women and the role food has played in the women's movement."

In the news business, you need something called a hook or a peg—a reason to write the story. It's even better if the reason has something to do with a recent event. That's news. In Marion's case, it was a new cookbook called *Learning to Cook*. It was her seventh, an attempt to teach the clueless how to make themselves a decent meal. Her targets were people who thought "toss apples in a bowl" meant throwing the fruit across the kitchen. To these people, "blanch" was the female lead in *A Streetcar Named Desire* and "working quickly" was perhaps the most terrifying phrase a recipe could contain. Substitute cornstarch for flour? Well, why not? They look the same.

I pulled into Marion's driveway, turned off my Barbie truck and tried to compose myself. On a good day in Bay Area traffic, you could make the drive in an hour or so. Mine had taken almost two. My back was damp with sweat. I was so flustered I left the headlights on, a move that would eventually involve a tow truck and an awkward end to the day. I said a goofy little prayer, a habit I had picked up from the people who helped me get sober. Basically, it went like this: "Help."

I stepped into the hot spring sun and walked to the back door, past a little cottage where her housekeeper or a family friend sometimes stayed. Suddenly, I felt optimistic. Certain moments in Northern California will do that to you. Your head will be all jangly and then you look up and catch a glimpse of the Pacific Ocean or notice a scrub oak bathed in the dreamy afternoon light that only California can produce and everything feels better. I looked at her yard, full of golden-green mustard plants. Someone rode a horse down a path nearby. I knocked on the door of her low-slung ranch house.

"Well, hello, dear," Marion said. She was seventy-seven then. Her blond hair had grayed, but it was in the same ponytail she had worn for years. She was tall and still fit, with hands that felt as strong and soft as walnut shells. I followed her down the long hallway to the kitchen, making fast mental notes of the snapshots that hung crooked and dusty in a long series of cheap frames. Marion and Ruth Reichl. Marion and Danny Kaye. Marion and Alice Waters. Marion and Edna Lewis. Marion and James Beard.

I am so screwed, I thought.

Just across her kitchen counter was a long wooden table where she held court. I sat down, and she offered me a sugar cookie from a pile on a plate. They were the simplest things. Just a pure expression of flour, butter, vanilla, sugar and egg. The coffee was plain and not too strong, made in an inexpensive white automatic drip machine on her cramped kitchen counter. The rest of the kitchen was as functional and plain as the coffeepot. Save for a copper-bottomed pan and a bottle or two of fancy olive oil (gifts from an admiring food pilgrim, no doubt), there was nothing at all remarkable in that kitchen. The electric range. The cheap paper towels. The store-brand dish soap. This was the same woman who liked to drive the Jaguar she'd bought with book royalties to the local Safeway every day and peer into other people's baskets just to keep up with how the folks who weren't eating at the fancy restaurants she went to every week fed themselves.

"Now what are you going to do with that?" she'd ask, staring down at a pork roast or bunch of kale. The astonished shopper sometimes recognized her, or if they didn't they'd treat her like a kindly aunt. You couldn't help but warm to her.

As the sun softened across the kitchen table, we talked about her deep concern for the poor souls who want to cook but can't.

"It's very tempting when we are old to become a missionary, to see the world as lacking," she said. "I really don't want to be guilty of that. I don't want to be preachy. But I wish there were a national law that made everyone cook steadily for two months. Then, if they don't like it, they can quit."

I scribbled this in my notebook, thinking she was absolutely right. I kept the tape recorder running, too, trying to think of clever things to say. I wanted a story, of course, but I had that kind of desperate, special feeling that this was a moment I would always want to remember. The kind where you focus on it so hard that it slips away and you never really feel it. On the drive to her house, I had been thinking about what to ask her. The simple act of cooking and eating dinner together seemed to be increasingly rare. Why did she think this was? And what would happen to us because of it? Howard Weaver, the editor who ran the *Anchorage Daily News* while I was there, used to talk about the newspaper as a modern-day tribal fire. The paper was the place people gathered every day to share culture, to feel connected. I loved Howard Weaver, and I loved the work it took to put together Anchorage's daily tribal fire.

At Marion's table, it occurred to me that I had found a
new one.

"Don't you think the dinner table is really the modern-day tribal
fire?" I offered, thinking about my own family and our life at the
table. "Don't you think it's the place where everyone gathers to
share news of the day and build a culture?"

"Well, I suppose it is," she said. "I have always believed that the
catalyst for social interaction is cooking and eating together. Today,
strangers cook most of the food we eat. People are living like they
are in motels. They get fast food and take it home and turn on
the TV."

If things are going well during an interview, a golden moment
comes when you know you've got what you need to make a good
newspaper story. Before that moment comes, you're on edge. Your
mind is firing in all directions, trying to keep track of the answers
and the notes you're taking while shuffling through everything
you've crammed in your head about the subject. You try to keep
the person moving along, but the real juice of a story often comes
when you follow her down some unexpected path. Marion and I
had hit that moment, and I knew I had my story. We talked about
the magic lessons of the table, about how serving food family-style
teaches a child to share, to leave something for the next person.
How sitting next to someone and eating creates a kind of intimacy
and gently teaches the art of conversation and the importance of
community.

As the afternoon stretched out, we drifted away from the matter
at hand and started talking like good friends. I told her how I had
landed in San Francisco and about Alaska. I told her that the whole
move had been a little unnerving. Somehow, she must have known

things felt worse than merely "unnerving." I must have really seemed lost. So she told me the story of how she had remade herself just after she turned fifty, after her children were grown. Marion had long been a famous sufferer of agoraphobia. She had lived all her life in California and had never left the state.

"I was so terrified I couldn't even drive across the Bay Bridge," she said. The paranoia and agoraphobia and depression had been fueled by alcohol and life with a blowhard of a lawyer husband.

Wait. Alcohol?

"I used to carry a little bottle of gin around in my purse," she said.

This detail was a great comfort to me. If I were the kind of woman who carried a purse, there probably would have been a bottle in there. Maybe not gin, but certainly pinot noir. Or, in a pinch, really cheap vodka. I grinned. Marion was my kind of girl.

"One day, I just knew I had to give it up," she said. She was fifty-one years old.

For some drunks, it really is that simple. Don't get me wrong. This doesn't happen to everyone, and sometimes it happens and you can't see it for what it is. But for me, and for Marion, when the doorbell rang and help was just standing right there on the porch, we let it in. She started swimming. She quit smoking. And she began to venture out of her home and her neighborhood. Her husband told her that without a few cocktails, she was no fun. She made it all sound kind of light, but I can imagine the scenes that probably happened right at that table.

Another miracle happened to Marion in 1972, when a friend somehow talked her into going to Oregon so they could take a cooking class with James Beard. Her son bought her a plane ticket. It was the first flight she'd ever taken, and the first time she had ever left California.

"Something inside me told me I just had to go," she said.

By the late 1970s, James Beard was the bridge between the generation of American cooks who worshipped only the French culinary canon and the new food revolutionaries who, like him, adored regional American cooking. He was a food pimp of the highest order, offering endorsements for almost any food product and writing cookbook after cookbook. Through it all, he helped a new generation dedicated to what could be grown around them articulate what they were doing in their kitchens.

Like an itinerant food guru, James taught cooking classes up and down the West Coast and in New York. After a week with him in Oregon, Marion kept in touch, and in no time he beckoned her to stay by his side as he taught classes and held court. "He liked the sound of her voice," said Clark Wolf, a restaurant consultant who witnessed much of what happened in the Northern California food scene during that time. For the next eleven years, she served as his assistant. The two shared a love of home cooking in a world where restaurant food was increasingly replacing dinner at home. But they also developed that kind of maternal, codependent relationship that older women and gay men sometimes have. When James would be dismissive and just plain mean to people, Marion would smooth it all over and find a way to rephrase the point so people would actually listen.

If you've ever had any doubt that a good life can be built on making the most out of random little connections, Marion is your proof. James Beard suggested to Knopf editor Judith Jones that Marion rewrite the 1,849 recipes in the 1918 *Boston Cooking-School*

Cookbook, written by Fannie Farmer. From there, Marion went on to help launch a host of other people's culinary careers. She did it through spreading only the best gossip about the cooks and writers and shopkeepers she liked, and maybe some bad about the ones she didn't. She became, for a time, the most beloved food figure in California. If Alice Waters was the mother of California cuisine, Marion Cunningham was the adoring aunt, the one everyone called to share their news, knowing there would be nothing but praise coming through the other end of the phone.

"She's like the den mother of the food movement," Ruth Reichl told me once, just after she landed the job as editor of *Gourmet* magazine. Ruth, too, had her own Marion moment when the two were in a car on the Bay Bridge and Ruth learned that Marion shared her agoraphobia. Dozens—maybe even hundreds—of other people have had Marion moments, too. Marion might have had only one prescription for whatever problem someone brought to her, but it sure was the right one. And I was about to get it.

After that first meeting, I always made sure to catch some time with Marion when I could, and to sometimes write about her. I would find a way to sit next to her at a party so we could catch up. When I would call to chat about a recipe, I would sometimes end up on the phone for an hour. She would come to lunch at the *Chronicle* test kitchen, and we would talk. I heard stories from her in New York, where a bunch of us traveled to watch her get a lifetime achievement award from the James Beard Foundation. When I had a chance, I'd head back to Walnut Creek with a tape recorder. Each time I managed to pull out a little more about her and her family. Her parents were Italian immigrants. She loved California, where she lived her entire life. She was one of the few people left who still called her hometown Los ANN-gah-leez. She was a famous hypochondriac and never held one job for very long. Once, during World War II, she talked a friend into helping her run a Union gas station. They were completely outmatched by the tasks at hand. Marion liked to describe how her friend would only pretend to fill tires because she didn't know how to work the nozzle. She'd crouch beside cars and send a hiss of air through her teeth.

Still, she glossed over plenty. Why, I wanted to know, did her son barely speak to her? Why did her daughter always seem to be struggling, despite the sexy food jobs Marion would get her?

Marion was always polite but vague.

"When you grow up in a house with two alcoholics, terrible things can happen," she told me once.

I knew enough not to push. I had heard rumors of bad things happening in that house from people closer to her than I was. I wanted to know exactly what had happened, but I didn't have the heart to ask. Or the guts. Maybe I just didn't want to see another side of her. I was content with how she was making her amends, a pursuit she based in large part on taking most of the notable cooks and food writers in Northern California under her sober wing.

Marion became such a figure that each year on her birthday, some of the biggest names in American food would fight it out over how to throw her the best party ever. For her eightieth birthday party, in 2002, every horizontal surface of the casual café upstairs at Chez Panisse held a cake or a pyramid of tiny cream puffs or a plate of cookies. A collection of eighty of her friends—Michael Bauer, Clark Wolf, the baking author Flo Braker, Alice

and Ruth among them—decided, in classic overkill fashion, to re-
cruit every notable baker they knew to make Marion something
sweet. They swore there were eighty offerings for her eightieth birthday, but I had my doubts. I lost count around forty-five, somewhere between a layer cake and a croquembouche. Still, it was pretty
impressive.

For entertainment, David Tanis, the food writer and Chez
Panisse chef, sent a dispatch from Paris, where he was living. It was
a poem, a set of birthday couplets that captured some of the things
everyone loved best about her. He called it "Marion Cunningham's
Rhyming Wisdom: A Partial Listing."

1. I don't mind driving near or far
   Long as I've got my Jag-u-ar.

2. If you don't find waking up too awful
   Come on over for a waffle.

3. It's simple, really dear, not a chore
   I make the batter the night before.

4. My friends like fancy salt from France
   I say, give good old Morton's a chance.

5. As for pie dough, there's no mystery
   Crisco's earned its place in history.

6. If only folks would dare to risk it
   Dinner's better with a homemade biscuit.

7. James Beard always liked my cooking
    But he added things when I wasn't looking.

8. My dear, this cake is quite a treat
    I do think I'd make it a tad more sweet.

The four lines about the waffles are my favorites. Those waffles are perhaps the most enduring symbol of Marion. As often as they could, people with some connection to food who lived in Northern California or were in town for a visit would brag about having gone over to Marion's for waffles. It was a line in the sand. You were either someone who had gone to Marion's for waffles or you weren't. I ate her waffles only once. On a Sunday morning, I went to her house with Michael. We sat around the same table where I interviewed her that morning years earlier, when I was so new to California I couldn't even tell you where Sonoma was. The recipe she always used is from the Fannie Farmer cookbook. You make it with yeast, so a stay overnight in the refrigerator helps it develop a kind of malty flavor. They come out of the waffle iron crisp and airy.

Finally, I thought, I'm going to have one of Marion's waffles.

She poured out the batter while we all talked and tried to top each other's jokes. We ate thick, peppery slices of bacon she baked in the oven, a neat trick I still use. (Place the strips on a rack set over a lipped jelly-roll pan lined with foil. After about twenty minutes in a 400-degree oven, the bacon will be perfectly crisp and flat and neither your stovetop nor your oven will be coated with grease splatters.) It was a dreamy moment, being there with my boss, now a friend, at a table that years before scared the hell out of me.

I've really made it now, I thought.

Then I forked off a piece of waffle. They weren't as crisp as the ones I had been served in my imagination. The syrup was still cold from the refrigerator. The bacon could have used a little more time in the oven. Maybe I'm missing something, I thought. Maybe I really am a culinary dullard, and simply can't discern that critical aspect of Marion's waffle technique that has enchanted so many of the greatest people in the American food world. Then it occurred to me. I had just come too late to the party. Marion was past eighty when she made them for me. Already the mind that could once remember exactly where and when she had sipped her favorite cup of coffee in Rome had started the long, slow fade to black. In the next instant, I understood. It wasn't about the waffles at all. It was about what everyone who ever sat at Marion's table had felt.

That first day I met her, I started to cry when she told me she had quit drinking. Then I told her my dark secret: I was a fraud and an alcoholic and I was scared to death I would fail. Fail the interview. Fail the job. Fail my life. I would be a disappointment.

"Dear, you seem pretty terrific to me!" she said.

That was all it took. A statement as simple as her waffles.

After that first day, she became my instant champion. And for the rest of my time in San Francisco, until I left for New York and Alzheimer's sent Marion into a small group home not too far from that kitchen where we met, she was also my friend.

From Marion, I received one of what would become a series of life lessons from women who know how to cook. No matter where you find yourself in life, no matter how badly you stumble, you can start over.

And it will probably turn out just fine, dear.

The recipe she always used has appeared in her breakfast book and in dozens of publications. When my former editors at the *San Francisco Chronicle* did a twenty-year retrospective of the best recipes the newspaper had published, the waffles took top honor for 1989.

MARION'S RAISED WAFFLES

½ cup warm water
1 package active dry yeast
2 cups milk, warmed
½ cup butter, melted
1 teaspoon salt
1 teaspoon sugar
2 cups all-purpose flour
2 eggs
¼ teaspoon baking soda

1. Use a rather large mixing bowl—the batter will rise to double its original volume. Put the water in the mixing bowl and sprinkle in the yeast. Let stand for 5 minutes, until yeast dissolves.
2. Add the milk, butter, salt, sugar and flour to the yeast and beat until smooth and blended.
3. Cover the bowl with plastic wrap and let stand overnight at room temperature.

4. Just before cooking the waffles, beat in the eggs, add the baking soda and stir until well mixed. The batter will be very thin.

5. Cook on a very hot waffle iron, adding about $\frac{1}{3}$ cup batter per grid. Do not use a Belgian waffle maker. Bake until the waffles are golden and crisp to the touch.

NOTE: The leftover batter will keep for several days if you cover it and put it in the refrigerator.

Yield: *About 8 waffles, which keep nicely in a warm oven until they are all cooked and ready to serve. Of course, people like them hot off the iron, too.*

2

Lemonhead

I landed in California the way Dorothy crashed into Oz. Or maybe the way she would have landed if she had just come out of rehab. My last drink was only a few months behind me. The people who help other people recover from addiction say alcoholics stop growing emotionally when they start drinking in earnest. So I found myself in a new world with the emotional skill set of a fifteen-year-old and skin as tender as a baby hamster's.

Don't get me wrong. Life wasn't all that terrible. In fact, parts of it were better than they had ever been. It is shocking how awesome life can be when you just show up without a drink in your hand. Did you know the sun comes up every day, and in those first minutes of sunrise the sky looks pink and orange and then lemon yellow? And remembering every conversation? Turns out that's quite handy.

The essential puzzle I needed to solve was figuring out who I was as a sober person. And that meant deciding what I really liked and what I did simply out of habit or because I was too afraid to change or because I thought I was supposed to. I was rethinking everything, from how I interacted with my family and my girlfriend to the small things, like what I preferred for breakfast. All of this was, as you could imagine, particularly hard work. Fortunately, in Northern California, figuring out what I liked to eat would be the easy part. It was also good practice for the bigger internal knots I had to untie.

My self-education began in a cramped one-story rental house in the Berkeley flats. I was still in Alaska when my friend Bennett Brooks drove over to check it out for me. The place was a serious wreck, but he thought I was resourceful enough to turn it into something. So I signed the lease sight unseen. I had to. The housing market was tight, and I had no money to store my battered little collection of household goods. I had only a week's worth of couch surfing lined up. My Barbie SUV, slightly rusty and banged up from seven Alaska winters, was being shipped down by barge. Any extra money I had was going to pay off the huge credit-card debt I discovered I had amassed once I woke up from the haze I had been in toward the end of my drinking career. Things were tough.

But there was hope. I had my new job at the *Chronicle* and a house in Berkeley, the place where a thousand great food trends were launched. But like me, the house needed a lot of work. It was wrapped in brown plastic siding, parts of which the sun had bleached to a sickly gray. A peeling psychedelic mural with a mermaid-goddess theme covered every wall in the bathroom, obliterating the charm of the deep, old-fashioned tub. Only three burners on the grease-caked 1920s Detroit Jewel gas stove worked, and an old wooden shed in the backyard threatened to collapse every day.

Still, it had a few things going for it. For one, the house was a few short blocks away from a parking lot that serves as a kind of anchor for three places that are culinary powerhouses in their own charming, scruffy Berkeley way. There is Acme Bread Company, which Steve Sullivan, a former Chez Panisse baker, started in 1983. I would end up living off the walnut levain and sweet baguettes. Next door to it was Café Fanny, Alice Waters's tiny espresso shop named after her daughter. And next to that, Kermit Lynch's famous and quirky wine store.

(In case you were wondering, the wine store, initially, was like having a little devil's workshop nearby. I walked in once, became immediately and deeply enchanted with a bin of Châteauneuf-du-Pape and walked out. It would take a few more years before I learned how to stroll through a wine store without having it mess with my head.)

The little rental house had a couple of other attributes. The landlord didn't mind that I had brought along my dear dog Lucy, a smart mutt who could pass for a small, well-behaved black Lab. And if I was careful, I could afford the rent.

The first night there before my furniture showed up was one of the loneliest of my life. I had only a sleeping bag and my dog. It was the first time I had been alone for several years, and I had no glass of wine to soften the fear in my stomach. And I wasn't sure it was ever going to end. Oh, I had hopes. When I left Alaska, the plan was that the woman I had been living with there would eventually join me. We had been together for several years, both thinking it might be forever, when my addictions torpedoed things. Don't get me wrong. She liked a good night of tequila shots and dancing as much as I did. I just took things to extremes. I lied. I spent our money behind her back. I was a bad girlfriend.

When I finally came up for air, she wasn't so sure she wanted to give it another shot, so to speak. But she saw I was serious about being sober. And we really did have a ton of fun together. It helped that her parents lived in the Bay Area, and getting out of Alaska is never as easy as getting in. For people who don't want to stay in the Arctic forever, jumping when you get the chance makes a lot of sense. For those reasons, and some I'll never know, she agreed to join me. I left Alaska promising us a better life, and she said good-bye believing it. She would be in California in a few months, just after she tied up some loose ends. I knew there was a chance she would never come, but I busied myself fixing up the little wreck of a house and fantasizing about the New Improved Kim she would find when she arrived. If I could just make the nest attractive enough, everything would be perfect. I would be the best darn sober girlfriend ever. My byline would be in the paper on a regular basis. The bills would be paid on time. See? Everything would be great!

It was the magical thinking of a child. At night, when the house was dark and my dog was all I had to hold on to, I would cry. I was afraid. I was full of regret. I was lost. On more nights than not, I did what other people who had managed to quit drinking told me to do. I picked up the phone and called someone else who was sober. And I tried praying, although I was rusty and awkward. I'd beg whatever power had gotten me this far to help me through the night. "Please," I'd plead between sobs so jagged they startled the dog. "Let this work out. Let me feel better." Relief was all I knew to ask for. I was like a teenage girl praying to God not to be pregnant.

Of course, there were other issues at play. I had no perspective, for one thing. When two people break up, it's never black or white. I see now that it wasn't all me, that it takes two to screw up a relationship. But back then I was taking extra helpings of the blame. I just thought, This is all my fault and there has to be something I can do to fix it. So I bought paint. I scrubbed the kitchen. I dug up part of the yard and created the most prolific tomato garden I have had to date. In the light of day, my life felt like a dream someone more fortunate was having. And writing about food in San Francisco was beyond anything I could have imagined. What better place to figure out who I really was and what I really liked to do? Unlike Alaska, there was an ocean that was sometimes warm enough to dip a toe in. There were plenty of mountains that didn't require extensive mountaineering experience to hike. There were people from all over, a lot of them like me.

And there was, of course, food. Figuring out what I liked to eat turned out to be a brilliant organizing principle for sorting out who I was. From my earliest days at that black kitchen table, food had never let me down. I had to believe it wouldn't this time, either. Mix in the kind of need that drove me to fill my Girl Scout sash with badges that guaranteed approval, and I was off to the races. I started to eat.

There was so much to learn, and the ride was exhilarating. It was as if I was rediscovering what it felt like to eat the most basic foods. I figured out how to cook Dungeness crabs and how to order just the right dressing for my crab Louie at the old-fashioned seafood bar I loved on Polk Street. I discovered glory in a simple piece of chewy artisan bread and unsalted butter. I tasted vegetables so perfect they only needed the slightest application of heat, oil and salt. I tasted varieties of olives and grapes I had never heard of before. I was thrilled that chop suey was invented in San Francisco and learned the best places to order burritos in the Mission District, making sure they didn't add too much rice. There was so much food history here! I drank cappuccinos at the original Peet's coffee shop that inspired America's love of dark-roasted coffee, hung out with Chuck Williams in his office at the Williams-Sonoma headquarters and learned to love Green Goddess dressing, which was invented at the Palace Hotel in the 1920s.

And I fell in love with a Meyer lemon. Not really one lemon in particular, but the whole genre of citrus that is really a cross between a mandarin orange and a lemon and was imported from China in 1908 by an "agricultural explorer" for the Department of Agriculture named Frank Meyer. They grew like crazy in California, but were not much more than ornamental backyard lemons until Alice Waters started using them at Chez Panisse in the 1970s. The smell is much more appealing than the tart, one-note Eureka lemons you find piled up at the supermarket. The rich yellow peel is thinner and softer, too. They are lemons with personality.

Discoveries like that sustained me. When I ate for work, I nearly forgot all about the loneliness and anxiety that seemed to be my factory setting during that time. I was all charged up with what then was a new idea. I would create a beat that combined the culinary aspects of food with hard news and cultural analysis. I would report news, but news that began on the plate. This was the early 1990s. Michael Pollan was almost a decade away from publishing *The Omnivore's Dilemma*, and the concept of food miles, or considering the impact of how far your food has to travel to get to your plate, hadn't migrated from its British academic beginnings to American popular culture. Obesity was just beginning to be viewed as an epidemic, and the Berkeley school district had adopted the first public school policy in the nation that emphasized organic food in school lunches. We still had Julia Child around to look up to, and the Food Net-

work was not yet powerful enough to make stars out of Rachael Ray
and Bobby Flay. No one knew what trans fat was, and everyone
seemed to think the Atkins diet was going to transform how the
nation ate.

Things were about to bust open. I just didn't know it yet.

For decades, most of the food journalism at daily papers was
divided, generally speaking, into three camps (admittedly, these are
broad generalizations): rumpled Washington-based newsmen who
covered things like the Department of Agriculture, the Food and
Drug Administration and programs to feed the hungry; smart,
sensible women who edited the food pages, telling readers how
to shop, cook and entertain; and gay men who reviewed restaurants. A few national journalists were building bridges between
them, like Marian Burros at *The New York Times*. My idea was to
approach food in a new way. I would cover it as a serious news
beat, writing about policy, culture, economics and social issues,
but from the perspective of the eater and cook. California, always
on the front line of America's food revolution, was the best place
to make it happen. It was the kind of coverage that *San Francisco
Chronicle* executive editor Phil Bronstein wanted, and that Michael
Bauer and Miriam Morgan, the food editors there, were ready to
deliver.

But before we could all agree to the marriage, there had to be
some courtship.

A couple of months before I actually nailed down the job, I took
some vacation time and flew in from Alaska for a weeklong tryout.
I wrote a couple of stories and tried my hand at some editing tasks,
but the essential test was lunch with the two of them. When you go
out for a meal on a job interview in the food world, what you

eat and how you behave mean a lot more than if you were interviewing for a job, say, covering energy policy in Washington. All those rules about only ordering wine if the boss does and not ordering pasta so your little business suit doesn't get splattered are child's play. The job interview meal, for a food writer, is pretty much the whole show.

The restaurant they picked was Bizou, a Mediterranean café both earthy and stylish. Michael was a big fan of chef Loretta Keller, who ran the place. Michael threw it to me to order first.

"So what looks good?"

I looked up, startled. I had been trying to hide how intensely I had been studying the menu, hoping my nerves didn't show. But I had no way out, so I made my move quickly. Fresh grilled sardines to start. (Now, I am not really all that in love with sardines because they can be too fishy and they get mushy in the wrong hands. But I figured they'd be a gutsy order. Local and suggestive of a bold palate.) Next, I casually suggested the tempura green beans, a dish I hadn't seen before but had read about. A gamble, but a calculated one. They turned out to be one of Loretta Keller's signature dishes.

The rest of the lunch went well. By the end, it felt like we were pals. I had made them laugh, and we shared the same notions about what the job was going to be. So far, so good. But there was another hurdle. The next night I would have to go on a restaurant review with Michael and his partner. I knew enough to suck up to the boyfriend. And I would offer only a few pithy observations but not spend the entire night trying to out-critic the critic.

By the time Michael got the OK to hire me a few months later I had given up the juice for good, but that night we drank wine together. I carefully monitored how much I took in, limiting myself until I could get back to my hotel and drink the way I wanted. Somehow I made a good impression. By the end of the tryout, I knew I had the job.

I didn't know much about the food in Northern California when I showed up four months later, although I wasn't completely without a reasonable set of cooking skills or enough restaurant knowledge to make my way around a food story. I spent a lot of my time traveling to eat. And I'm no chef, but I can cook. If you ate my food, you'd leave the house happy. Still, I lacked any real cooking technique, save what I picked up through a few classes here and there and from the generous instruction of friends who were better in the kitchen than I was. Wine and cigarettes (the latter a delicious habit I had to later abandon, too) took a toll on my ability to taste. But I was fearless in the kitchen because, from the start, I was comfortable there. My mother saw to it. She had to feed seven people every day, and she had to make the meals work even within the budget constraints of a family where bill-paying night meant staying as far away from my father as possible.

"You never felt like we didn't have any money, did you?" she asked me years later.

I hadn't, but in retrospect, I realized our lunches never held the tiny, expensive bags of Fritos that came with the coveted (but completely racist) Frito Bandito erasers for the ends of our pencils. Instead, our potato chips were tucked into plastic sandwich bags with the fold-over tops that never kept them crunchy until lunch. I carried a paper bag instead of the Partridge Family lunchbox that I fantasized about. Some evenings, we faced liver and onions. It was cheap and made my father happy. When we had bacon we were each allowed only one piece. I figured out early that when there were only seven pieces of chicken, you better go in fast and early or you'd be left with the wing, which I still have a special fondness for largely because I often got stuck with it.

I never tasted a real Oreo until I started hanging out with kids whose parents didn't buy the store brand. When I noticed the difference, I acted as if I preferred the latter, immediately assuring myself a future in the competitive community of know-it-all food writers who make bullshitting each other about food a high art.

I also learned a lot by cooking for random social events, most notably my parents' loosely organized neighborhood cocktail parties. (One of my early specialties: Place a small mound of shredded Longhorn cheddar cheese and a single pickled jalapeno slice on individual Doritos that have been carefully arranged on a baking sheet. Slip into a hot oven until the cheese melts. Arrange on a platter and pass around to your parents' friends.)

I spent a summer waiting tables at a Mediterranean restaurant in Detroit, where the owners allowed me to work as many double shifts as I could take, despite the fact that I was still a teenager and dropped a dish of cream of broccoli soup on my first customer. That little bit of restaurant experience led to a job writing restaurant reviews at *The State News*, the college newspaper at Michigan State University, where I would eventually become the managing editor. Meanwhile, I still had to make rent. I cooked short-order breakfasts, waited tables and tossed pizzas. (Still, I was so broke during college that my first girlfriend and I had to stretch a box of something labeled "bacon ends and pieces" and a bag of egg noodles for a week.)

But what did I really know about food? Could I make beurre blanc? I couldn't even say it right. Could I keep up with San Francisco's chefs and make sense when I talked to a farmer? Well, no. Had I eaten all the great cuisines? Did I know what food at a three-star Michelin restaurant tasted like? Again, no. But I knew how to ask questions. And I was filled with a kind of desperate fear that was so strong I could see no other way to survive than putting my head down and plowing ahead no matter what. I had to discover what I liked, both in my heart and on my plate.

On a practical level, comparative tasting is a big part of a food journalist's job. If you can't taste critically, you can't write about food with any relevance. Maybe you are thinking this is not so hard to do. Everyone eats, right? Figuring out if one steak tastes better than another is not like trying to split an atom or rewire a house. That's true, to a degree. But unless you taste a lot of examples of something, and you're thoughtful while you do it, it's hard to be very clear about what you like and don't like, about what's good and what isn't and why. This was what I had to learn how to do, and fast.

But it soon became clear that if I wasn't careful, I could become one of the overeducated food snobs who were already trying to one-up me instead of a smart, openhearted eater, which is what I wanted to be. Chris Kimball, who started *Cook's Illustrated* but also its much more entertaining and quirky, old-fashioned cousin called *Cook's Country* magazine, wrote about the difference between un-adulterated joy and its more controlled and intellectual cousin, pleasure: "As kids, we didn't have to describe the experience, didn't need adjectives to tell our story. We just gulped down the Nehi or started at one end of the chocolate bar and kept going until it had slid home. We didn't share. We didn't compare notes. We didn't have to tell the story of how something tasted."

It's like James Beard used to say, "A hot dog or a truffle. Good is good."

I got my first lessons in professional tasting early on at the *Chronicle*, where the editors were fanatics about recipe testing. Interns from the California Culinary Academy would rush dishes from a test kitchen to a counter near the editor's desk, and we would all hurry over, forks in hand. The bad stuff would go to the sports department. (A truism of any media organization: Almost all food will be eaten, no matter the quality, if left near the sports department.)

In the beginning, I hung back a lot and watched. Did Michael like it? Did one of the other writers with the big, fancy culinary degrees like it? And how did my own tastes compare? Often, we all agreed that a particular dish was good. But sometimes I pretended I liked the recipe if everyone else did. At least in the beginning. I'm not proud of it, but I was so unsure of myself I couldn't risk looking like the idiot I felt I was.

They didn't let me hang out in the back row for long, though. My first big story was to be a sweeping review of boxed chocolates for Valentine's Day. When Miriam Morgan, the long-standing editor of the food section, told me about the assignment, I quickly went back to my desk and hid the Kit Kat wrapper. Surely, this could sink me. Now, you are probably thinking, "It's a bunch of chocolates. How hard can this be?" Actually, pretty hard.

To taste well, you have to know something about cooking and how certain ingredients interact with each other. I learned this during that chocolate tasting. We ended up sampling more than four hundred pieces of chocolate over the course of four days. One of those days, after we had spent the morning eating chocolates, the interns brought in a dish of braised rabbit in a sauce whose main feature was grainy mustard. The dish was horrible, all out of balance. I got brave.

"Can we cut back on the mustard?" I asked. "I'm choking on it."

Everyone agreed with me. I was a beaming beacon of food writing fabulousness. Then Michael weighed in.

"We need to retest this in the morning."

It wasn't the recipe, he explained. We had all eaten too much chocolate. The sugar had altered our palate so the mustard tasted too sharp. The exact same rabbit recipe tested out perfectly the next day.

The other thing I learned during those first months at the *Chronicle* was the importance of extensive tasting. You have to build a catalogue of food memories. To understand good chocolate, you have to know bad chocolate, and you should experience them side by side. It's a method that has helped me through the years, whether I am tasting water, salt, milk, ground beef or any other food that might not seem to have much variation. Once you set examples of something side by side and begin to really think about them, huge differences emerge.

So if you haven't eaten a Hershey bar next to a piece of perfect Michel Cluizel chocolate that melts at a point just about the temperature of the roof of your mouth, and you haven't been able to tease out nuances of vanilla or tobacco or dried mango, then you might not believe me when I say that the Hershey bar tastes like sour, grainy earwax. Or at least what I imagine earwax might taste like. But there is a caveat here, and that is taste memory and context. My mother used to make a chocolate cake for my birthday that had pieces of broken Hershey bars suspended in whipped cream for frosting. I love that cake, and I have tried to re-create it with fancy-pants chocolate. It's never as good.

I feel that way about a lot of food. I like things that would make food sophisticates immediately cross me off their lists. California Dip, for example. At least once or twice during football season, I like to mix up a bowl of dip made with Lipton onion soup mix and serve it with a bag of rippled chips. And I sometimes like to put a bowl out at a casual cocktail party (yes, ex-drunks can throw cocktail parties). Try it once. You will be amazed when it is one of the first things to go.

I worried that the dip was the kind of food quirk I might have to abandon to impress my new food friends in San Francisco. Or I would have to reimagine it, spending hours making a proper demi-glace with veal bones from grass-fed cattle. I would be forced to caramelize organic onions and fold them into some crème fraîche from a small local dairy, then gently fry local potatoes in peanut oil and sprinkle them with a bit of sea salt. But the dish would never be what I wanted, especially during football season. And I was starting to see that listening to my inner chip-eater—trusting what I liked—was the only thing that was going to work.

One day I was talking about taste memories with Clark Wolf, who ran the Oakville Grocery way back when the store was doing for the West Coast what Zabar's and Dean & DeLuca were doing for the East. He has tasted food with all kinds of people, James Beard, Julia Child and Robert Mondavi among them.

"How do you measure what's appealing, what you really think is good to eat?" I asked him.

"It's all about having a good set of benchmarks," he said.

That is, one must have eaten a perfect example of something to understand how every other example of that recipe or piece of fruit or slice of cheese measures up. Like a lot of food people, he collects benchmark tastes the way others collect birds for their life lists. The problem is you can never taste everything, but you can have enough benchmark tastes of the right foods to build a decent palate. The key, he says, is knowing what you need to taste and what you can take a pass on.

"I don't want to know how to taste Pringles," he said. "There is not enough time in the world to learn to taste nature, you know? Why waste it on something that is so far from nature?"

"But I sort of like Pringles," I told him.

"Oh, me too," he said. "But only alone in a hotel room."

This was a great comfort to me. Even a die-hard professional eater can be a closet Pringles man if you scratch the surface. I was going to be OK.

So here are some basic things I learned in my quest to figure out what I liked and didn't like when it came to food. The first thing is to simply say yes or no. Do I like it or not? It's an all-guts, no-brain call. And if I do, why? This is where the intellectual and emotional work comes in. Why is one cheese better than another? Is it because it is a perfect example of how that particular cheese is supposed to be made? Or does it appeal on some other level? Does the creaminess and funk change how you feel? Does it remind you of mushrooms? Does it bring up memories of the first perfectly grilled cheddar cheese sandwich you ever had? And can you separate the appeal of memory from the actual quality of the food?

Like that Hershey bar cake, I have a particular fondness for cube steak. They sell some made from tough little cuts of pasture-raised beef sirloin at our food co-op in Brooklyn. Every once in a while I pick up a couple, sprinkle them with salt and pepper and a little adobo seasoning, dip them in flour and slip them into a pan of hot olive oil. Sometimes I go all out and make chicken fried steak with a little cream gravy from the pan drippings. Either way, they are only a little different from what my mother used to make on a Tuesday night, and they remind me of a midweek culinary simplicity that meant life was safe, steady and predictable. But to Marlena Spieler, a food writer friend, they are traumatic. Her mother baked cube steaks, green beans and tomato into a grim casserole that she insisted the children finish.

"I hated this dish—and she made it about once a week!" she said in a long e-mail she sent on the subject. "It smacked of everything bad: tough gray meat, lower middle class never having anything delightful, unstylishness, grimness and duty rather than enjoyment, of doing what you're told to do rather than what you wish or think is good, and of not being listened to."

That's the thing about food. How good a dish is depends a lot on what one brings to it. Once, I sat in an extended tasting of root beers. I realized I was most attracted to the ones that tasted like the spices my mother uses to make ginger snaps. The bottles I liked least reminded me of Pepto-Bismol, which reminded me of being sick.

A fter a few months on the job, I was beginning to sort out what I liked. I'd already eaten a dozen cheeses I had never seen before and fresh fava beans and the best bread of my life. I was coming of age as an eater. I was also learning how to write more intelligently about food, and how to take care of myself. That mostly consisted of playing as much softball as I could and talking to other people who used to drink too much but who had found a way to solve their problem.

And I learned how to be a better cook. California cooking, with its produce and bright, clean flavors, is the style I still love the most. Vegetables in all kinds of shapes and colors, the flavor a grill imparts, good olive oil, citrus, bread with character and uncomplicated but skillfully made cheeses—these are the basics of a Northern California pantry and the tastes I always return to. And of all the flavors of Northern California that I sampled during my quest to learn what I like, the Meyer lemon is at the heart. I still ask friends and family for regular shipments of Meyer lemons. I buy them when I see them here in New York, which isn't often. They are ridiculously expensive here, so friends sneak them out of people's yards and bring them when they visit. Even today, all I need to do is run my thumbnail over the thin skin of a Meyer lemon and I am instantly back in the Bay Area, a sober kid fresh off the grill from Alaska, unsure about who I was and what I liked, but thrilled at the chance for a new life.

Meyer lemons are my touchstone. They help me remember to be mindful of where I came from and what I like.

The woman from Alaska did come live with me in the falling-down Berkeley house. But it didn't take a marriage counselor to see that it couldn't work. Our fights were loud and frequent, and no matter what the fight seemed to be about, it always came down to this: she was unhappy with her life in the city and still angry about what I had become in Alaska. I still felt guilty and responsible and insecure. We finally saw that the only way either of us could live the lives we wanted was to end it. So she took her dog and moved to the mountains near Lake Tahoe. My dog, Lucy, and I moved in with a friend from work who had a big, rambling house in Oakland.

By this point, I had been in California for a couple of years. I was newly single. It was time to take stock: I had made it out of Alaska and through the early years of not drinking. I was thriving at work, and I was even having fun again. I was starting to shake those debilitating feelings of guilt and shame over my addictions for good, but I was still feeling lonely and a little sorry for myself. I was convinced I knew absolutely nothing about love, and that having a relationship that lasted more than four or five years was out of my reach. My parents had managed to do it for more than fifty years. What was wrong with me?

A big Meyer lemon tree grew in the backyard of that post-breakup house in Oakland. Twice a year, the soft yellow fruit would pop out from between the waxy green leaves in such volume that after my roommate and I juiced as many as we could, we hauled grocery bags full of fruit to the office just so the lemons wouldn't rot in the grass. One afternoon, not too long after my ex-girlfriend and the U-Haul had left for the mountains, I found a photograph of us from our days in Alaska. We were on skis, our dogs panting by our sides. I took it out to the backyard and I sat under that Meyer lemon tree for most of the afternoon. I thought about what my life used to be like, and what it might be. I realized I finally knew what I liked, both for my plate and my heart. No one else could have taught me those lessons but me. Because until you know what you really like, you're lost.

I buried that photograph under the lemon tree, and then I went inside and made a lemon pie.

———

This is a good thing to make even if you have only a few Meyer lemons. It's from Lindsey Shere, a pastry chef who got her start at Chez Panisse. You can use any pie crust you like, but you might try one from Marion Cunningham if you don't have a reliable recipe. The one I've included here is written for people who swear they can't make pie crust. Sometimes I make one with butter, fresh lard or even coconut oil, but Marion's is foolproof.

MEYER LEMON MERINGUE PIE

THE FILLING
2 large Meyer lemons
2 eggs
3 egg yolks
6 tablespoons sugar
3 tablespoons salted butter, cut in 3 pieces
3 tablespoons unsalted butter, cut in 3 pieces

THE MERINGUE
3 egg whites, at warm room temperature
¼ teaspoon cream of tartar
6 tablespoons superfine sugar
½ teaspoon vanilla extract

1. Once you have the crust in the pie pan, edges crimped and bottom pricked with a fork, freeze it for 20 to 30 minutes.

2. Prepare the filling by grating the zest from the lemons into a bowl. Strain in the lemon juice, then press through as much lemon pulp as possible.

3. In a heavy saucepan, beat the eggs, yolks and sugar until just mixed. Stir in the lemon juice and pulp, then the six tablespoons of butter.

4. Cook, stirring constantly, over low to medium heat until the mixture comes together and thickens enough to coat a spoon. Remove from heat, allow to stand 5 minutes, then whisk briefly to smooth. Set aside.

5. Preheat the oven to 375 degrees. Line the frozen shell with aluminum foil, weight with beans or pie weights and bake for 20 minutes, or until set and dry looking. Remove the weights and foil, turn the heat down to 350 degrees and continue baking until shell is golden brown, about 12 to 15 minutes. Set aside and allow to cool slightly, but leave the oven on.

6. Spread the prepared filling in the shell and bake for 10 to 15 minutes or until the filling is just set. Remove pie and turn oven to 375 degrees.

7. Make the meringue by beating the egg whites until frothy, add the cream of tartar and continue beating until rounded peaks form. Beat in sugar and vanilla.

8. Spread the meringue over the filling, making sure it meets the edges of the crust to make a seal. Swirl in a design with a spatula and bake for about 10 minutes, or until the meringue is lightly browned.

9. Allow to cool completely, but do not refrigerate.

MARION CUNNINGHAM'S NO FEAR PIE CRUST
(for a 9-inch crust)

1¼ cups all-purpose white flour

¼ teaspoon salt

⅓ cup vegetable shortening (trans fat–free, of course, or for a flaky crust, ⅓ cup cold butter)

¼ cup very cold water, or a little more

1. Combine the flour and salt in a large mixing bowl.
2. Fill a ⅓-cup measure with shortening. Scoop the shortening out of the cup with your fingers and put it in the bowl with the flour. Rub some flour on your hands, then roll the shortening around in the flour so the fat isn't too sticky to handle.
3. Break the shortening into 4 or 5 smaller pieces and coat them all with the flour in the bowl. Now lightly rub small pieces of the shortening and the flour together with your fingers for about a minute to make little lumps. If there is loose flour at the bottom of the bowl, scoop it up to the top with your fingers and rub shortening into it to make more lumps.
4. Continue scooping up and rubbing, working lightly, letting the bits of shortening fall back into the bowl. When most of the flour and shortening have been transformed into lots of little lumps and the dough looks like grated cheese, you've mixed enough.
5. Sprinkle the cold water over the dough and stir with a fork all around the sides and bottom of the bowl so no dry flour

remains hidden. Stir until the water is mixed into the flour and has disappeared. Reach down to the very bottom of the bowl and gather up all the dough. Pat and press the dough until you have a ball of dough. If some of it is still so dry that pieces fall away, sprinkle that area with a little more water and gently press and pull the dough apart, sprinkling a little more water on it. Pat it into a ball again.

6. Sprinkle a large cutting board or a countertop lightly with a small handful of flour. Spread the flour into a circle bigger than your 9-inch pie pan. Put the dough in the center of the circle of flour. Flour the rolling pin. Flatten the dough a little with the pin, then begin rolling from the center out to the edges to make a circle. Don't roll back and forth. Move the dough now and then to make sure it isn't sticking.

7. If it is sticking, slide a metal spatula in a wiggling motion under the dough to loosen it. Sprinkle more flour on the surface, then continue to roll the dough into a big circle, about 1-½ inches larger all around than your pie pan. To make sure, put the pie pan upside down in the center of the dough and check that your circle is about the right size. The dough will be about as thin as a cracker.

8. Roll the dough around the rolling pin. Lift the pin up and center it over the pie pan, then unroll the dough into the pan with the fold in the center of the pan. Now unfold the dough against the inside of the pan and pat the dough all around the inside edge to fit snugly.

9. Fold the hanging dough back up onto the rim to make a double thickness of dough around the edge of the pan. Be

careful not to tuck the dough under the edge of the pan, which would make it hard to dislodge after baking.

10. When you have neatly folded the dough all around the edges, press indentations into the dough, squeezing the edges together, to make a scalloped edge. Prick the bottom surface of the crust with a fork and proceed with a filling recipe.

3

Leftovers from the Revolution

One of the smartest things I did when I arrived from Alaska to start work at the *San Francisco Chronicle* was call my good friend Bennett to give me a little tour of where he liked to eat and shop for food.

Bennett, who is quite a thoughtful cook, picked me up at my crummy little rental house one Saturday morning. The first stop on our food tour would be Café Fanny, an espresso and egg bar Alice Waters had set up so she had somewhere to go for breakfast. It's a slip of a place with a short counter. Outside on the patio and along the rim of the parking lot she set out wrought-iron tables so people could sit and enjoy a perfect bowl of café au lait made with extra-creamy Clover organic milk or a simple soft-boiled egg served in an egg cup. I would end up with an almost unnatural love of the garlic-rubbed levain bread just warm enough for a couple of prosciutto di Parma slices set on top to offer up their hammy aroma.

But it takes a certain perspective to appreciate an expensive coffee shop whose tables are in a parking lot. I brought my parents there one morning when they were visiting from Colorado. We sat on shaky little bistro chairs with a line of customers filtering past.

Dogs panted under tables or waited, tied to posts, while their owners ran into the Acme Bread Company next door for a baguette. My
dad picked up the tab. It was pricey for a man who appreciates a
restaurant where two eggs sunny side up and a side of hash browns
costs $3. He still tells the story when asked what it's like to eat out
with his food-writing daughter.

"Geez," he'll say, building to the triumphant punch line, "it was
sixty-five dollars to eat some eggs in a parking lot with dogs crapping
all over!" I still cringe a little every time. I so wanted him to love
what I love, to be proud of a daughter who had figured out where
to get the best café au lait in Northern California. I hadn't yet
become secure enough in my own preferences to not worry if they
didn't mesh with my father's.

Bennett continued his tour. There was the little Japanese fish
market on San Pablo, with its shad roe and Pacific oysters, and
Monterey Market, where I would return frequently to buy $11-
a-pound chanterelles and my weight in heirloom tomatoes and
gypsy peppers. We looped past the original Peet's coffee on Walnut
Street, and the maddening Cheese Board, a collectively run and
carefully curated cheese shop that began in the 1960s and is based
on the Israeli kibbutz model.

The finale of our tour was a drive past Chez Panisse, the temple
of California cuisine, the ground zero of goat cheese and mesclun
greens, the restaurant that made farmers into rock stars.

"Well," Bennett said as he idled in front of 1517 Shattuck
Avenue, "there it is." My heart sank. It seemed so plain. Shattuck is
not a particularly lovely street, and the restaurant does nothing to
announce itself. In 1971, a bunch of amateur carpenters remodeled
a house and made it Chez Panisse. The outside is covered by trees.

The name is hand-painted on a curved wooden sign at the entrance. Off to one side, a small ramp leads to a rabbit warren of closets and porches and hallways where produce is delivered and salami is hung and tomatoes are stored on racks. It's also the back door to the kitchen and the gateway to the offices. In front, a week's worth of menus is tacked up behind glass in a wood case. An evening's supper might look something like this:

An aperitif

Chino Ranch vegetable salad with wild mushrooms

Dungeness crab chowder with fennel and herbs

*Grilled rack and loin of Magruder Ranch veal
with potato cake and a garden salad*

Almond praline ice cream crêpe with poached pear

A few months after Bennett's tour, I sat down in the dining room at Chez Panisse for the first time. It hadn't been that long since I had walked into the *San Francisco Chronicle* and picked up a reporter's notebook. I figured that if I was going to write about food in Northern California, I had better eat at the temple. One can only imagine the thrill that snakes through a girl who survived her teenage years on a diet of Bob Seger, White Castle sliders and weed when she finds herself sitting at Chez Panisse.

It was a small, quiet lagoon of white tablecloths and Craftsman architecture with every detail just so, down to the copper sconces and the thoughtfully casual lettering on the menu. Pedestal bowls held morel mushrooms and artichokes. The open kitchen with its big cooking fireplace was one of the first of its kind in this country. Diners could watch cooks stir bouillabaisse and, on the long work table that ran the length of the kitchen, set slices of apricot tart on plates. Upstairs in the café, where the vibe is a little more frantic and the tables are without cloths, the menu might feature $25 plates of Bolinas goat shoulder braised with thyme and white wine served on a little bed of turnips and artichokes or pizzas from a wood-fired oven with little charred bits and a crisp-tender crust that might hold wild nettles and pecorino. Rounds of goat cheese in crunchy breadcrumb coats nestled against lightly dressed, garden lettuces. The dish, which would be copied in cafés all over America, got its start here. Alice brought the idea with her from France, buying goat cheese from a neophyte cheese maker named Laura Chenel and all sorts of interesting lettuces from people who agreed to plant a little patch near a driveway or on some land they were cultivating as a counterculture statement.

Downstairs, our meal was going to be a little more formal, but still sourced and footnoted in a way that made you feel like you had personal relationships with the dozens of men and women who produced the food. People mock it now, but it was radical then.

We were just into the main course when I overheard the host talking to a waiter.

"Alice is here."

I turned toward the open kitchen, where quiet chefs solemnly plated our next course, and watched her glide through on her way toward us in the dining room.

"Johnny needs a flashlight," Alice said to someone who had appeared near the host stand. Then she adjusted the contents of a pedestal bowl.

We all stopped, forkfuls of lamb and peas in midair. Behind her, lumbering through with a stain on his striped shirt, was the man who would be sleeping in her little Provençal-style guest cottage that night: Johnny Apple, the late, great *New York Times* chief correspondent, former head of seven different *Times* news bureaus, the newspaper's lead reporter on the Vietnam War, chronicler of ten presidential elections, the man whose byline appeared on the front page seventy-three times the first year he worked at the paper and, lately, grand cultural commentator and prodigious chronicler of meals. He had what my colleagues and I believed to be the biggest expense account in the history of food journalism. Mr. Apple would later help me get a job at his newspaper, but at the time I just kept thinking, That's Johnny freakin' Apple! I didn't know enough at the time to say, "That's Alice freakin' Waters."

The buildup to dinner at Chez Panisse is huge. But unless one is prepared, the first time can be underwhelming. You sit down to a few nuts and a little aperitif, move into a plate of raw halibut and then a pile of greens, pork and shelling beans. The meal ends with a little dish of peach ice milk and the bill is $95 before the tax, drinks and the automatic 18 percent gratuity. For some people, the only reasonable response is, "What the hell?"

In a way, my first meal there reminded me of when I was five and my mother brought my little brother, Kris, home from the hospital. For three days, ever since I'd woken up and seen my parents' empty bed, I sat by the window, crazy with excitement over what promised to be the cutest baby I could ever imagine. My mother swooped in, a Russian-style fur hat on her head to protect against the damp gray of a Michigan January, and a bundle in her arms.

She set it carefully on the bed and peeled back the blanket. There was my little brother, wrinkled, scaly, red and crying. Disgusting. I turned and left the room.

Eating that first meal at Chez Panisse was not quite that disappointing, but it was in the same emotional family. Just as I didn't yet understand why a baby was magic or how cool my brother was going to end up being, I didn't know enough about Alice's food and what it took to appreciate it. The more you know about where the food comes from, the greater the pleasure. It takes patience and dedication, two things I had never been very good at.

Before I landed in San Francisco, I relied, like most people, on culinary pyrotechnics or nostalgia-inducing home-style recipes or simple salt and sugar to get pleasure from a meal. But eventually, over meals at Alice's and other restaurants like hers, my expectation of what food could be was lifted. When I ate one of those soft, dark Black Sphinx dates Alice is so fond of and peeled a little pixie tangerine from the Ojai Valley, its perfume exactly what you might think sunshine smelled like, my brain adjusted itself. There is a purity of flavor, a truth, to the food at Chez Panisse. A slice of raw halibut is clean and light—almost a whisper of fish. A piece of pork shoulder from a well-raised animal is luscious, the flesh piggy and complex. After a few meals like that, I discovered how happy I could be when I could connect what I ate directly to a ranch or a farm or the woods. This is not to say I don't appreciate what a great chef can do, what high art cooking can be. That's a thing unto itself. All I am saying is that I don't need a lot of fancy-Nancy food to be happy.

In the grand culinary world, all the fawning that seems to envelop Alice and her restaurant contributes to a sentiment among some food critics, both professional and recreational, that the place just isn't all that. It's a particularly popular pastime among a certain segment of food bloggers. Still, a half dozen years ago, *Gourmet* magazine deemed Chez Panisse the best restaurant in the world. It was quite controversial. Michael Bauer, the editor who decided to take a chance on my pasty Alaskan self, always gives it his highest ranking in the *San Francisco Chronicle*. Then he feels defensive about it.

"Each time I survey the four-star restaurants, I feel that I need to justify why Chez Panisse should be among them," he wrote in the paper a few years ago. "The ingredients are superior to those you'll find anywhere in the country, and the staff treats them with such care that each bite is a revelation. To me, that's the perfect definition of a four-star restaurant."

In the decade that followed my first meal at Chez Panisse, Alice became a good source and a friend of sorts. That's never an easy mix in journalism, but you can't be a decent food journalist and not have her on your source list, and after so many years you develop a relationship. We have shared a handful of meals, one of which was in a peach orchard and ended with each of one hundred guests getting one perfect whole Cal Red peach served naked on a plate. We have conducted dozens of interviews and had dozens of other gossipy, informal conversations. Sometimes she drives me crazy with her wispy, dreamy dramatics.

"Well, Kim, my dear," she might say. "We just *must* get Obama to understand the pleasures of the table."

Or this. "When I see what children are eating, well, I just want to cry."

But usually, she articulates such a sense of hope and inspiration that I hang up the phone absolutely convinced I need to completely change the way I live. The girl who made a big bowl of California onion dip and sometimes snuck out for a Jack in the Box taco must be stopped. (My commitment never lasts long, though.) Still, Alice does have an effect. How could she not? She can be the most maddening person to talk to, and the most enlightening. Once I asked her if she really thought changing the way we feed children at school was possible. The federal system for feeding schoolchildren is a $12 billion federal program deeply tied to government policies that help subsidize large agricultural operations. More than thirty-one million kids eat that government-subsidized food at school and most districts get less than $3 a meal. Given that, food like chicken nuggets, beef crumbles and the cheapest frozen pizza imaginable made from commodity food seems like the only way to fill the bellies of millions of children who might not be getting full meals at any other time of the day.

Alice didn't blink. In her world, the answer was obvious, simple and completely achievable: "We need a total dispensation from the president of the United States who will say, 'We need a curriculum in the public school system that teaches our kids, from the time they are very little, about food and where food comes from. And we want to buy food from local people in every community to rebuild the agriculture."

She is absolutely convinced it could happen if the leadership would just decide to make it so.

"This is what it's going to take," she told me. "Just like physical education came into the school way backa when."

On one hand you think, Yeah, right. And they're going to melt down all the cruise missiles and turn them into wood-burning pizza ovens for every elementary school, too. Still, somewhere in the back of your mind, you realize that is exactly what needs to happen. Imagine if students learned math by laying out garden plots and biology and earth science lessons were taught as students prepared soil, gauged the weather and harvested food. Grinding maize could be the basis for a lesson on pre-Columbian civilizations. Recipe writing might become an English lesson. Digging weeds and building fences would count as physical education.

It became fashionable, in the "Spring of Obama," to trash Alice for elitism or for claiming to have started the whole modern food revolution. Maybe some of her critics—many of whom are deep into sustainable agriculture and nose-to-tail eating—are the equivalent of angry teenagers going through a phase of hating their parents. To me, their criticism seems unfair. Alice is quite aware that she runs a restaurant where the food costs a lot of money and that her worldview is that of a privileged white woman, but she works hard to broaden her perspective. She thinks quite a bit about how to get good food to people without the means to eat at places like Chez Panisse. And I have never heard her claim to be responsible for the food revolution.

The thing is, when Alice started Chez Panisse in 1971, she had no intention of becoming anything other than the owner of a restaurant where she could eat like she wanted to. Her streamlined philosophy—that the most political act we can commit is to eat delicious food that is produced in a way that is sustainable, that doesn't exploit workers and is eaten slowly and with reverence—wasn't anything she could have articulated when she was running around Berkeley's University of California campus in vintage dresses.

Once, years later, when Alice was in my house cooking lunch for a story I was writing for *The New York Times*, she said she was envious of my relationship with my wife, Katia Hetter, who was pregnant with our daughter at the time. "Falling in love changes everything, simply everything," she told me. "That's what happened to me when I went to France. I fell in love. And if you fall in love, well, then everything is easy."

When she was in college, Alice had traveled and worked for a time as a Montessori teacher in France. When she returned, she craved the little lettuces and tiny red strawberries because they were what she tasted while she was there. Her restaurant came out of that craving. She was pretty much a privileged girl from New Jersey who came into her own at the University of California–Berkeley just when the Free Speech Movement was at its apex and she simply wanted a lovely place to hang out and watch the revolution.

At the time, food was very political, but not in the way it is now. There was no deep appreciation of deliciousness. This was the era when thousands of hippies were brewing Evening in Missoula herbal tea in their bamboo strainers, making bad yogurt and baking bread whose heft and density were an indication you were serious about your politics. And among the many problems that come with an organic dirt farm run by stoned revolutionaries with little understanding of agriculture is this: They can't grow very good food. Once she had tasted French cooking, Alice decided that no revolution was worth food that tasted so bad.

"Alice started the restaurant as a retreat from politics," Ruth Reichl told me early on in my California education.

Alice was a pretty young flirt—you might even call her a party girl. But she had a seriousness of purpose, a need for control and a bunch of friends who were deep into film and free speech and politics. She talked some of them into helping her start the restaurant, which they named after the most generous, open-hearted character in a French film trilogy by Marcel Pagnol. Her dad floated her $10,000. There were other investors, too.

Alice, who was twenty-seven, hired a lot of her friends, especially people with little bits of food experience, or sometimes none, to keep things interesting. The first dinner cost $3.95. Diners, many of whom waited endlessly for their meal, received pâté, a farm-raised local duck braised with olives and a plum tart. Everyone was paid the same. "The notion was that people should have good lives," Ruth told me.

Alice was a terrible businesswoman. Some nights, she would plunk herself down on a plastic bucket in the kitchen and cry over the unpaid bills. She and her unlikely band of Free Speech Movement loyalists spent the first decade of Chez Panisse getting high, discussing film and politics and sleeping with one another. In the first year alone, $30,000 worth of wine was unaccounted for, according to David Kamp, who writes a clear-eyed, funny and detailed slice of Chez Panisse history in his book *The United States of Arugula*.

That no one really knew how to cook was not much of an issue. Over the years, Alice figured out that the key to success was hiring people who cooked better than she did. Especially once she got famous, she ended up taking several public slugs to the gut, some from former chefs who went on to be stars in their own right, some from the old-school chefs of France and the stylists of New York's kitchens who said she was little more than a really good grocery shopper and argued that olive oil isn't really a sauce. But she never pretended to be a great chef, and in fact she stopped cooking in the kitchen twenty years ago. She just wanted people to be as transformed by food as she was.

Especially in the last decade, that idea has been picked up and massaged by thousands of diners, cooks and farmers along the way. It has caught on because in the wake of a half century of a steady march toward an industrialized farming system and away from the traditional family dinner table, people are hungry for the kind of satisfaction that comes from food grown and prepared simply. Once, when she was just beginning to work on reforming school lunches and before she had picked up on the messages of Michael Pollan and Carlo Petrini, the charismatic Italian who started the political-gastronomic movement called Slow Food, she told me that if you change how people eat, you change a nation.

I thought it was the most idealistic and ridiculous thing I'd ever heard.

"And how is that supposed to work?" I asked.

"The way we live now shuts down your senses," she said. "Nobody wants to smell anything; nobody wants to feel anything. You don't want to feel any pain. You don't want to smell anything bad. You're living in a very narrow range and you're eating in a very narrow range. You're eating two or three or five or ten kinds of things. It limits our thinking about everything in the world, about simply everything. About art and culture and war. That's why we have to open up and eat differently."

I had to work to get my head around that. Is she saying that if we all just had the right attitude about food there would be no more war? Bring out the unicorns!

The power and the madness of Alice is that she operates outside of the reality-based system most of us use. She has a way of demanding things that seemingly can't be done, then imploring people to help make whatever unlikely event she is dreaming of happen because it is simply the best way to do it. Although she is very sensitive and loyal to a fault, she's often oblivious to the rubble that falls around her as she marches on. She gets something in her head, and she's just going to stick with it no matter what.

In her personal life, it means she has slept with cooks at the restaurant, some of them, like Jeremiah Tower, quite famously. She has broken hearts and had hers broken. At the restaurant, it caused much difficulty in the running of things. A cook might explain why the pork can't be roasted in the way she wants and still be done in time for service, and she won't hear of it. Certain guests must be accommodated when there simply isn't room. People must be fired immediately or hired immediately. Still, she has a kind of low-burning patience. She plays the long game very well, adhering to the first part of Winston Churchill's famous saying: "Never give in—never, never, never, never, in nothing, great or small, large or petty, never give in."

Of course, that phrase had a second part, which she is less likely to consider: "Except to convictions of honour and good sense."

Her need to stick to her vision of how things ought to be trickles down even to friendships. I saw this when I interviewed Marion Cunningham and Alice Waters for a piece on friendship for the *Chronicle* Sunday magazine. Marion had long been a kind of beloved older sister to Alice. She's the one who knew all her secrets, all the loves and all the heartbreaks. In the course of the conversation, it became clear that lettuce was a point of contention. Waters loves tiny, perfect garden lettuces almost to a fetish. She hates iceberg lettuce, which Cunningham loves.

"Keep in mind I do love farmers' markets and what Alice has done," Marion said as I sat with the two at Alice's house in Berkeley. "All you have to do is eat at Chez Panisse and you know you aren't doing it right. But iceberg is meaningful to me. Alice has tried to reform my eating and buying habits in very tactful ways, but somehow I haven't changed very well."

Waters patiently countered.

"It's not that I don't like the idea and appreciate the qualities of some iceberg lettuce, but what I object to is the way that commercial farmers have produced it and stored it and sold it to the American public. And the kinds of dressings they are encouraged to pour all over it to mask the fact that it can be old and overgrown," she said.

I wonder aloud if she could just maybe make an exception for her friend. That maybe she could see that someone's taste for something could be valid, even if it didn't match hers.

Not so much, apparently.

"I know Marion is clinging to a taste, the way that she ate it way backa when," Alice said. "Well, way backa when was before the war and before big commercial farmers took hold of it and it was a loose head of lettuce with a wonderfully crunchy flavor to it."

Now, iceberg symbolizes all that is wrong with American food production, Waters said.

"It is omnipresent. It doesn't have a season. It doesn't have a sense of place."

She just couldn't have her friend eating it. But she also wasn't without some sympathy for Marion's tastes. So on her seventy-ninth birthday, Alice gave her friend fifteen little crisp French lettuce heads. They had the same watery iceberg crunch but with a seasonal and organic aesthetic. Marion, of course, told her they were delicious, but, out of Alice's earshot, she admitted they tasted not at all like iceberg.

"I hate that Alice has had to work so many years to get me to do the right thing," Marion said. "But she doesn't give up. That's the thing about her. For thirty years Alice has not given up on one true thing she believes in. And I have been a test."

Even now, with all the power Alice has amassed as an icon, she will not let it rest. Not so long ago, I met Alice in the green room at the Times Center, where she was going to be interviewed onstage by the editor of *The New York Times Magazine*. The annual food edition had just come out, the meat of which was an 8,000-word article by Michael Pollan making a clear, honest case for an overhaul of the American food system. The article was called "Farmer in Chief." It was directed squarely at President Barack Obama. The entire issue could not have existed even a decade ago. It was such a symbol of the progress that has been made. But it was not perfect.

Alice picked it up the minute I walked backstage and waved it around. She had turned to the page where Deborah Solomon interviewed Robert Kenner, who directed *Food, Inc.*, an indictment of most of the food in the grocery store. In it, he admitted he is a big Trader Joe's fan. "I love their walnuts," he said, "and if you toast them, they're delicious on yogurt."

"Kim, did you see this?" Alice said to me. "He doesn't get it! He still just doesn't get it." In Alice's world, big chains with cheap food whose real costs are hidden are part of the problem.

Once, during a period in which she was trying to explain why every school in the nation should have a curriculum based on the garden and the kitchen, I asked her if maybe that bar was a little too high, given that the country couldn't even figure out how to teach basic math and English. Could there be a compromise?

"I am not a compromiser," she said. "Certain things are just too important to compromise on. I just cannot compromise on what children are fed in school. I can compromise on the kinds of food they eat. I cannot compromise on the purity and nutrition and tastiness of the food. Children should have the very best of everything."

But, I counter, is the government responsible for that?

"I don't think we can consider lunch outside of the domain of public responsibility. Even the most temporary shortfall in nutrition has profound implications in a child's ability to learn. Most of what we're doing are perfectly normal things that until very recently children were involved in. It's not like we're trying to teach Swahili. These are things humankind has known how to do. Cooking and growing food."

This is Alice Waters, the woman who has not sold out, who has not started a Chez Panisse Las Vegas or sold a special line of mortar and pestles or cloche hats. Who has endured lots of love affairs, both fruitful and humiliating, who believes that if she just writes the right kind of personal note she can finally get an organic garden planted on the lawn of the White House. (And she did. Michelle Obama dug one up a few months after her husband took office. She didn't credit Alice directly, but I promise you the garden is there in good part because of her.) Even when people mock her wispy ways and roll their eyes at her unblinking, idealistic beliefs and grumble that she always claims the credit, she gets hurt but she doesn't stop. She remains the most ridiculously uncompromising, true-blue person I have ever met in the food world.

"I'm just an optimist of the first order," she told me. "I just got dipped in Berkeley in 1964 and I believe." And over the years, she has come to show me that an unwavering hand on the rudder, coupled with patience, can change things. No matter what anyone says.

Now, let me tell you about the time I saw her underwear and she nearly saw a domestic meltdown at my house. It all happened the same day, almost ten years after I first watched her swoop into Chez

Panisse. I had moved east to write for *The New York Times*. Alice agreed to meet me at the Greenmarket at Union Square so I could write a story about her and her new cookbook. This is the biggest of the seventy or so farmers' markets that are woven into the city. Some, like the ones trying to get a foothold up in Harlem, are three or four stands. But Union Square is where they started, and after thirty years it has evolved into such a varied collection of vendors selling meat, bread and vegetables that even the most uninspired person couldn't walk away without a new idea about something to eat.

This would be a fine place, I thought, to ask Alice to meet me. My plan was to walk her around the Greenmarket and shop for lunch. Then we would schlep all of our finds back to my apartment on the first floor of an old brownstone in Brooklyn and cook. I wanted to show people how simple and easy it was to prepare food from the Greenmarket. A photographer and a video crew from the paper would meet us.

I popped up from the subway and there she was, a tiny Berkeley lady with a big woven shopping basket in her hand.

"Well, hello, my dear," she said.

It was New York hot and I was already sweating like Nixon. I leaned down and gave her the double-kiss thing you have to do with some people. (I'm always clumsy with it. For a while I tried to enforce only single kissing, but that was even more awkward.)

After our graceless greeting, she immediately ordered me behind a tent. The *Times* video journalist assigned to the story needed Alice to put a microphone and its wireless power pack somewhere on her petite body. Because the day was so hot, we'd all worn the flimsiest clothes we could. Alice was draped in an airy purple top and a thin brown skirt that fell to her knees. Of course, this left no pockets and no waistband for the power pack. We struggled to find a place to put it, trying parts of her blouse. Then she turned her back to me, hiked up her soft little skirt and said, "Let's try this." This was not exactly one of the great moments in journalism I dreamed I might have when I joined the *Times*. But Alice is a can-do girl, and I took inspiration from her lead. I bent over and figured out pretty quickly that the microphone pack would only drag down her panties.

"Alice," I said. "I don't think this is going to work."

At about the same time, we eyed her big, sturdy market basket. We tossed the radio pack in the bottom, attached the microphone to her blouse and off we went, hoping for the best.

The shopping went well, but Alice was stopped enough times to make it a long trip.

"Are you . . . ? Are you . . . ?" a man stammered.

"Yes, I'm Alice."

"I just want to thank you for everything you've done."

A woman from a little home-style restaurant in Greenpoint, Brooklyn, bravely walked up to say hello, her words tumbling out as she tried to explain that everything she does, everything in the kitchen, is done with the sensibility inspired by Alice.

"Well, I would love to come and visit your restaurant," Alice told her.

"Please don't," the woman said. "If you come in, we'd probably lose it."

After a couple of hours, we had a huge haul, and I was getting worried about how we were going to turn it into lunch let alone a story for the newspaper. Simply having Alice Waters come to your house is enough to keep you up at night. It's like the time your parents invited your second-grade teacher over for dinner. You suddenly see everything through her eyes. And I immediately thought, I live in a dump. I worried about the Diet Pepsi in the refrigerator;

the package of Lipton onion soup mix in the cupboard and whether the three kinds of olive oil I had would be good enough. (Not to worry. She brought her own.)

The other factor was Katia. She's a journalist herself, and a very good sport. I have forced her to drive many miles out of our way to squish through a muddy field just to talk to a goat farmer or make a special stop to eat a small, greasy cheeseburger at an old roadside stand someone told me about.

"Isn't this the best cheeseburger you've ever had?" I'd say.

"Well, it's good," she'd say gamely.

"Wait, you just have to taste this coconut ice cream. Isn't it amazing?"

"Well, it's good," she'd say.

"Try this cheese. Don't the nettles make it sublime?"

"Well," she'd say, "it's good."

Katia was going to have lunch with us that day, mostly to keep me from freaking out. I should mention two other things about Katia here. One, she was four months pregnant with our daughter, Samantha, at the time and was eating like a linebacker. (Artificial insemination, if you were wondering.) And two, she's got a touch of hypoglycemia, which means she has to have a good hit of protein in her stomach every few hours. So when I say, "Is it okay if we make one quick stop so I can check out this kebab place?" she will invariably say yes. This is a food writer's dream partner.

She had asked only one thing of me as I headed out the door that morning. "Just make sure you call before you get in the cab to come here, OK?"

"Sure," I said. "See you around noon."

Did I remember to call? No. By the time we had gotten through the market, filmed the segments, endured the Alice worshippers and packed into the trunk of a cab several bags filled with hyssop and thyme and basil and runner beans and tomatoes and eggs and peaches and golden raspberries, I forgot that one detail.

I made it through the two front doors in our building and eased open the one to our apartment.

"Katia, honey, we're here!"

No response. She must be getting dressed, I thought.

The muggy day was hovering around 85 degrees. We were all parched and I wanted to get something cool to drink in Alice's hand quickly. I figured we'd unload our haul on the dining room table, and while Alice was sorting through it I could go back to the kitchen and tell Katia we were ready for drinks. Then I'd head back and help everyone get settled.

We set our bags down and Alice requested the loveliest platters I had to display it all. I pulled some from the dining room shelves and then went back to find Katia. I smelled something cooking and looked in the toaster oven. Sizzling along nicely were a half dozen chicken nuggets and some frozen French fries. OK, at least the nuggets were Bell & Evans, the most natural version you can buy. The French fries were organic, too. We had purchased them both at the Brooklyn food co-op where we worked every month. But it didn't matter. Alice Waters was in my house and chicken nuggets were cooking in my toaster oven.

I heard something in the bathroom and threw open the door. Katia was standing in the tub, dripping wet.

"What are you *doing?*" I hissed.

"Why didn't you call?" she spit back, her eyes blazing.

It was like the married lesbian version of Lucy and Ethel having lunch, and Alice Waters was our Bill Holden. Katia figured we would be preparing something with no meat, and she was right.

Aioli, boiled eggs and vegetables were the centerpiece. She needed protein, and she was pregnant, so she indulged one of her pregnancy cravings. She figured she'd take a quick bath, down a nugget or two and be good to go when I called to say we were heading back from the market. Except I had forgotten to call.

We jumped into action. She threw on a robe, whipped out of the bathroom and headed to the kitchen, leaving little puddles of bathwater on the hallway tile. She pulled the offending items from the toaster oven and snuck into the bedroom to choke a few down and get dressed. I grabbed some glasses and a pitcher of ice water and went back to the front of the house to stall.

Alice was sitting at the table, looking at all she had purchased and talking on the phone to her daughter, Fanny.

"Oh, it's so lovely," she was saying. "We have the most beautiful tomatoes, and peaches, these tiny lovely peaches . . ."

Saved by the beautiful produce once again.

Alice went on to work hard for two straight hours in my little kitchen, making us a beautiful lunch. We pitched in as directed, creating this menu:

*Eggs, soft-boiled for about six minutes, their yolks just
barely holding together.*

*Three kinds of beans, including a little pile of fresh shell beans she
simmered in salted water with some thyme.*

Small, soft summer potatoes and artichokes.

A glimmering bowl of olive green aioli made by hand.

*Thick slices of miche toasted in the toaster oven, which had
already gotten plenty of use that day.*

*Sliced peaches, nectarines, red raspberries, strawberries and blueberries
covered in a little chilled syrup made from boiled golden raspberries.*

A friend she had brought along for her own moral and physical
support moved the picnic table in our backyard across the bluestone
and out of the sun. Eric Asimov, the great *Times* wine writer whose
desk is behind mine at the paper, had given me a bottle of French
Viogner, which I poured for them. I sat back, ate, and I was happy.
At that moment, I saw that the life I was starting to have was the life
I wanted. I hadn't given up. I had been patient. Just as it had with
Alice over so many years, perseverance was starting to pay off.

———

This is a version of the aioli Alice made for us that day at my house.
Like all good things, it takes a little patience and a little persistence.
But it's worth it.

ALICE'S AIOLI

2 or 3 small garlic cloves
A pinch of salt
1 egg
½ teaspoon of water
1 cup olive oil

1. Pound the garlic and the salt in a mortar and pestle until
   it's smooth.

2. Separate the egg and add the yolk to a mixing bowl. Find something else to do with the egg white.

3. Add about half the garlic and the water and mix well with a whisk.

4. Using a cup with a spout, dribble the olive oil into the egg yolk mixture, whisking constantly. It helps to wrap a damp kitchen towel around the base of the bowl to keep it from moving. Or have a friend pour while you whisk.

5. As the sauce thickens and lightens in color, add the oil a little faster but keep whisking.

6. Taste and add more of the salt and garlic mixture. If it's too thick, thin it with water.

· 4 ·

Popular Girls

Here's the thing I was starting to understand about life. Just when you get the boat on course and the water seems calm, a storm comes up. In my case, it was a series of little storms. I had solved the big problems. I had stopped drinking and I had started to believe in myself again. And just those two things in and of themselves were pretty exhausting—enough, really, to call it a day. But once the big layers got pulled back, I got to see all the more subtle wrinkles that I would need to iron out if I was going to be happy.

One big wrinkle came in the form of Ruth Reichl. Walking into the world of food writing was like going to a new, competitive high school. The New York writers were the most popular kids in school, and Ruth Reichl was their leader. If I was going to survive, I had to find a way to claim a seat at their lunch table.

I had one brief, glorious run as a popular girl in the early 1970s, when life was all Pixy Stix and slumber parties. Me and my girls ruled Thornbranch Avenue, one of several cul-de-sacs that punctuated a new subdivision on the western edge of Houston. My mom had a tricked-out shag flip that approximated Florence Henderson's in her later Brady Brunch period. Her hairdo, like the orange and lime green pop art flowers in our breakfast nook, fit perfectly with the times. The Texas suburb we lived in reflected all the promise and grooviness of the era, tempered by the safety of corporate jobs, smooth new driveways and instant pudding. Chrissy Evert was the new hot teen tennis star, and her aunt lived right across the street. People were flowing into the state at a rate of about 55,000 a year. Our family was among them, plopped down like aliens from the Midwest into the land of barbecued brisket and oil rigs and shiny new Neiman Marcus stores.

I was fully engaged in the carefree life of a child in the 1970s, when a girl could travel without seat belts, play on the street until well after dark and purchase Tareyton cigarettes for her dad without one question from the man at the Stop-n-Go. We felt invincible, running out the screen door every morning with the kind of free- dom I would crave the rest of my life. We climbed onto our banana seats, grabbed the chopper handlebars and rode without worry, leav- ing our bikes on the front lawns when it got dark, knowing they'd be there in the morning. Baskin-Robbins had just invented pink bubble gum ice cream, and because children hadn't started getting obese at alarming rates, our mothers happily took us to the new McDonald's up the road as a treat when the grind of nightly home- cooked meals was just too much. We built forts in the woods with abandoned lumber from the new construction that was slowly eat- ing up the fields on the edges of the city, never wondering who else might be hiding among the little stands of pine trees. We swam in a neighborhood lake, jumping out whenever anyone yelled "snake!" to avoid a water moccasin bite. And if there was ever any trouble, I had two big brothers to protect me—when and if I could get their attention.

These were heady, heady times for a preteen girl with a posse. But they were bad times for a girl I'll call Karen.

Karen lived at the end of our street. She was a dark-haired kid who carried a maroon satchel and walked to the bus stop each morning reading a book. She was the object of our scorn, the bottom of our block's popular-girl hierarchy. And the torture we put her through was in full effect on my eleventh birthday.

For birthdays, my parents gave each of their five kids a choice of celebrations: dinner out with a friend at the fanciest restaurant you could think of or a slumber party, usually convened in one of my dad's musty camping tents pitched in the backyard. Soon enough, the appeal of a fancy salad bar and prime rib would win out. But early on, it was no contest. Slumber party. This particular year, we decided to move the party across the street to Michelle's house.

Michelle was pretty and smart and had young parents who seemed much cooler than mine. She had only an older sister, which meant her house was always much quieter than mine. Ours was more organized and active. There was always something cooking and always something to do. Michelle liked to come over and get caught up in the swirl. I liked to go to her house because no one was around and her mother bought brand-name junk food and cereal with too much sugar.

My mother insisted that we invite Karen to my party. I was sure she would ruin everything, especially my reputation as the coolest girl on the block. No matter how much we protested, there was no way around it. I think Karen must have known what was in store for her, so she showed up that night thinking a clever piece of offense would be her best defense. She had somehow gotten her hands on *Sound Magazine*, the latest Partridge Family album. We grabbed it, put it on the record player and then proceeded to actively ignore her for the next twelve hours. We danced the crazy dances that preteen girls dance. We had a contest to see who could stuff the most potato chips in her mouth. We giggled and whispered and gossiped and double-dared each other. But we made sure we didn't include Karen.

My enduring memory of that party is Karen taking her record album, crawling inside her sleeping bag and sobbing. Even now, it makes my stomach turn. I Google her name, wondering how weird it would be if I called her to apologize.

What I didn't know at the time was that I would never again be one of the popular girls. In fact, I would soon enough become the one who wanted to crawl to the bottom of her sleeping bag.

This first became apparent when I entered high school. At the end of eighth grade, my father picked up the family and moved us from the wild, swinging suburbs of a young Houston to the old-money land of Top-Siders and jowly GM executives in Grosse Pointe, Michigan. As a freshman with a Texas drawl, a family station wagon paneled in vinyl faux wood and a growing suspicion that I might like girls more than boys, I was easy prey for the popular, mean girls of Grosse Pointe.

My parents wouldn't be much help. Mom had her hands full trying to find pediatricians and shoe stores and distribute children to three different schools every day. Dad was a new executive at a tire factory on the east side of Detroit, trying to keep the unions under control and coming home late, his suit smelling like pencils and rubber. I was on my own. And that feeling that I would never measure up, that the cool girls would always be cooler, took over for good.

Which brings me to Ruth Reichl.

There is no getting around the fact that Ruth Reichl, former *New York Times* restaurant critic and, until 2009 when the magazine folded, the air-brushed editor in chief of *Gourmet* magazine, is the popular girl of my professional life. When I first decided that food would be a good way to make a living, I had no idea I would eventually be sitting at her old desk at *The New York Times*, more tortured by her than ever. Or that over some very expensive sushi (thank you very much, Condé Nast!) I would finally figure out why girls pummel other girls, why we always measure ourselves against one another and what it takes to make it stop.

I first met Ruth Reichl at seven A.M. in the lobby of the Campton Place hotel in San Francisco. A week earlier, Michael, my editor, had walked over to my desk with an assignment. Ruth was coming back to the Bay Area for the homecoming queen's triumphant return as the nation's most important food critic and smash author. I was to trail her all day and write about her promotional efforts for the second of what would eventually be a flood of memoirs. Finally, I would get to hang with the popular girl!

The owners of the hotel had given Ruth use of the $1,800-a-night suite, with its limestone bathroom, silk curtains, four-poster featherbed and a view of Union Square. She took the elevator down and slid across the lobby like a cat.

"Hello, I'm Ruth," she said, extending her hand.

Well, yes, you are.

Her yearly Condé Nast clothing allowance alone was more than three times my annual salary, but here she was dressed in a soft, silky Chinese-style jacket with a mandarin collar. Chinatown chic. "I need to get some tampons," she said. "Can you excuse me?"

I sat back down to wait, sure I was experiencing the most awkward beginning of an interview ever. And from that day on, whenever I was anywhere near her, I would feel as awkward and incompetent as a high school freshman in last year's jeans. She became my kryptonite, rendering my wit and casual, breezy conversational skills worthless.

When I first started writing about food full-time, I quickly discovered that everything I wanted to do, she had already done or done better. Every place I wanted to go, she had been, and it had all been fabulous. For years I would measure myself against her, and I never measured up. Some people call this a role model.

R uth was born in New York City in 1948. She grew up in a Greenwich Village apartment and a suburban country home. She came of age as a food writer in California, specifically Berkeley, which is where I was living when I first met her that day at the Campton Place hotel. Her food writing break came when Colman Andrews, who would soon become her lover, hired her to write restaurant reviews for *New West* magazine. She used a wild, fanciful and sometimes novelistic approach that included ginned-up bits of dialogue. Her style, though often criticized, would eventually help break down the stodgy, formal structure the genre had come to rely on. Ruth would have to tame the embellishment when she became the food critic at the *Los Angeles Times*, and later *The New York Times*. Newspaper editors have this thing about not knowingly printing fiction. She fell in line, of course, but she was and is, above all else, more literary than journalistic. Although many people still have a deep dislike of her, both for what can seem an imperious aura and for her elastic treatment of fact, plenty of people (me included) admire that she changed the nature of restaurant reviewing in this country permanently and for the better. She opened up food writing to a world in which love, angst, joy—essentially all of life—could be played out over a good, steamy pot-au-feu.

She was in her last year of writing restaurant reviews for *The New York Times* when we met that day in the lobby. During her tenure there, she was both loved and hated, as most critics anywhere are. Her particular angle was a kind of democratization of the more formal French-leaning restaurant criticism that had been invented and perfected at the *Times*.

Ruth used a kind of proletarian, experience-based literary style. She pushed the form, stretching it in the way new American chefs at the time were changing what it meant to eat out in this country. It certainly pushed the boundaries of reportage, although she would go to great lengths to understand whether a dish was prepared according to the correct culinary canon. She made high art of wearing costumes that allowed her to find out how single old women or sexy blond women might be treated. Molly was shy, and as a result got badly treated by a condescending staff. Chloe, who was as hot a blond as Ruth could make herself up to be, got better tables. Ruth was a new kind of everywoman restaurant critic, weaving class and gender into her reviews, which often read like little short stories.

In 1993, she famously dined at Le Cirque as shy Molly. She was ignored and humiliated, forced to wait forever for a bad table and then treated with scorn by the waiters. Then she went back as herself, the famous restaurant critic. Sirio Maccioni, Le Cirque's owner, kissed her ass but good. Ruth knocked the place down to three stars. It was genius.

She told *Salon* magazine how she got the idea: She was having dinner with *Times* editor and then London bureau chief Warren Hoge, the man who had hired her. He made the reservation in his own name, because he didn't think anyone at the restaurant would know him.

"They seated us at this apparently not-good table," she said in the interview. "Halfway through the meal, Sirio came rushing over. He didn't recognize Warren, but somebody had said to him, 'That's Warren Hoge.'"

He wanted to move them.

"He said, 'So-and-so just said, 'How could you seat Warren Hoge behind the glass?' It was shameless. It was like, 'We've given you a bad seat; we've made a terrible mistake; please let us move you.'"

She stayed put and exploited the event to wonderful effect.

Her role as the everywoman diner didn't make everyone happy, of course. Hard-core food people felt she was too loopy and ethereal. None was so steamed as Bryan Miller, the lover of things French who had done the job before her. He complained to the *Times* editors that Ruth was ruining the system that he, Craig Claiborne and Mimi Sheraton, past critics, had worked so hard to establish.

"How do you think she comes off giving SoHo noodle shops two and three stars?" Miller wrote in an internal memo that got leaked to the New York press. (For the record and to her credit, Mimi Sheraton, one of the great shoe-leather food reporters of her day and the *Times* restaurant critic for much of the 1970s and early 1980s, came forward to say she didn't agree with him.)

Ruth would later write a book about her six years at *The New York Times* in the third installment of her memoirs, called *Garlic and Sapphires: The Secret Life of a Critic in Disguise.* I had been at the newspaper less than a year when it came out. Inside the building, at least among the people I was working with, the book was largely ignored or actively reviled. She had used a much-loved and deceased secretary as her sidekick, creating entire scenes and dialogue with the woman in a way a lot of people felt was disrespectful. She stuck it to an overbearing top editor, who used Ruth's name to get reservations—an ethically questionable practice at most newspapers and especially at the *Times*.

Turns out he was an amalgam, as were many of the people and the events in the book. That approach didn't sit well with folks who base their livelihoods and their reputations on not making stuff up. And at a place where you pledge a kind of unspoken allegiance to the institution and where protocol dictates polite respect for one's coworkers (at least to outsiders), the book did not play well among my new colleagues.

Some of the criticism of Ruth, I think, comes from her general demeanor. Those who have known her a long time say it gets more fanciful and fabulous with each passing year. As David Kamp wrote when he reviewed *Garlic* for the *Times*, "Reichl's acute self-satisfaction can, at times, cloy to the point where you're tempted to grab her by that lustrous mane and whirl her into Alice Waters's wood-burning pizza oven."

But, he points out, "the flip side of all that onanistic mmm-ing and ahh-ing is a genuinely infectious enthusiasm; when she discovers the ideal soba noodles—which, upon being slurped up, 'vibrated as if playing inaudible music' in her mouth—you want to be right there with her in the Japanese noodle parlor, exchanging sultry glances over the steaming broth."

When I first arrived in California and her book *Tender at the Bone* came out, I had no perspective about my own conflicted feelings about Ruth or the confidence to apply any kind of critical assessment of her work. Instead, I latched on to that book like I was thirteen and had just discovered a world where girls could fall in love with handsome vampires who would always protect them. I was back to being a lost adolescent who longed to be part of things, to be cool, to be anything but what I was. I studied everything about that book, hoping it might offer some clue about how I was supposed to navigate the strange world I had found myself in: a newly sober food writer in the land of what seemed at the time to be all milk and honey. (Maybe not honey. Ruth hates honey.)

In the mornings, as I rode the BART train from the flatlands in Berkeley under the bay to the *Chronicle* offices in San Francisco, I would read a chapter in her book and think how I was way out of my league. She moved with such ease through the world I had just stumbled into. And she wrote about it a lot better than I did, too. Who did I think I was? Once again, I felt like the kid my dad threw in the water with water skis. There is no way I can do this, I thought. I am just not good enough.

But I knew there was no climbing back in the boat until I learned how to ski.

I was shocked that Ruth exposed so much in that book, and like everyone else who read it, I of course felt like I knew her personally when I finished it. I learned that her mother was a manic-depressive, and that Ruth spent much of her childhood trying to keep her mother from poisoning people with rotten food. I learned how she herself felt like a fringe player around Alice Waters, who was just starting Chez Panisse.

I knew I was a different kind of writer than she was, more of a notebook and boots-on-the-ground kind of reporter who viewed her job as explaining things—as factually as possible—to the people who have invested a few quarters to buy a newspaper. But that didn't keep me from comparing myself to her. It's what we do, especially,

I think, as women. We pull out the measuring stick as a way to figure out where we stand in some kind of social hierarchy. Maybe it's
because we can never really win in a world dominated by men, so
we become especially critical of ourselves and other women. It's the
arena in which we stand a chance at victory. But why we need that
victory is really the heart of the question.

I'm no anthropologist, and I'm no feminist scholar. But I do
know there were a thousand ways I didn't compare to Ruth. Here
are some of them:

She spoke French, of course. I butcher it so badly that I get completely ignored in Paris and, worse, must endure the disappointed
looks of coworkers who somehow expect more from someone at
my level.

She had obsessive, romantic adventures in places like Tunis and
Naples and Tuscany and Paris, and can seemingly recount each perfect morsel she has ever put in her mouth. I have traveled to some
interesting places, sure. Ate great pho in Vietnam and slippery, delicious pelmeni in strange towns in the Russian Far East and whale
fat in remote villages in Alaska. But these were grueling, budget
adventures or hurried newspaper assignments with no room for
anything but the business at hand. There were no magical encounters with the one person left making the one kind of wine that is
the best kind of wine ever in the whole world. There were no tran-
scendent moments over bowls of noodles. I slept on school floors
and in dollar-a-night guesthouses. Ruth slept in villas with big beds
and fluffy white sheets, getting lost for days with a new lover.

I'm not going to lie to you. I got a little obsessed with Ruth in a
Single White Female kind of way. One day I drove up and down
Channing Way in Berkeley, searching for her old house where she
lived in rooms painted wild colors with her artist lover and dozens

of other characters. I pored over her stories of fights with her house-mates over whether to use refined white sugar, and how she became one of the early "freegans," diving into garbage bins for food. I fantasized about having an important life filled with soul-wrenching debates over how to achieve social change. I tried to imagine the woman who at the time was the most powerful restaurant critic in the world as a young, frizzy-haired hippy writer and cook who was so self-assured in her culinary nerdiness that she entitled her first book (written in 1971 when she was unemployed and living in New York) MMMMMM, *a Feastiary.*

Even after I made it to *The New York Times* myself, I couldn't stop the comparisons. She had graduated from the University of Michigan with a degree in sociology and a master's degree in the history of art. I was a Michigan State University dropout who spent all my time at the college daily instead of in class. And remember my little battle with the goods in Kermit Lynch's wine shop in Berkeley? Ruth had no such battles. She marched right into that very same wine shop and, after several more visits and despite her later claims that she felt intimidated, walked out with an invitation to go to France with him on his next buying trip.

Ruth courted the man who would become her husband in M. F. K. Fisher's house in Sonoma, using a picnic basket packed by the late, great food writer and a walk to a magical waterfall and pool as her seduction tools. On my first date with Katia, I took her to a restaurant where I kind of knew the chef and got a free appetizer.

Even years later, when I had had a child and was well established in New York, she was still so much better than me. We were eating lunch and I confessed to her that my beautiful baby girl had rolled off the bed and onto the floor. It was a horrifying moment. I heard a thump, then a yelp. I rushed into the bedroom and found the baby crying on the floor, hysterical but unhurt. I was terrified.

"I am officially the worst parent in the world," I told Ruth.

"Oh, that's nothing," Ruth said. Then she proceeded to tell me about the night she had her young son in the back of a cab without a seat belt. A car hit the cab and her son's head slammed against the Plexiglas that divided the driver from the passengers.

"There was blood everywhere," she said.

Even in moments of bad parenting, Ruth outdid me.

Back when I was waiting for her to get tampons, if you had told me that one day I would become friends with her and that I would be living in New York as a parent and *Times*woman, I would have thought you were nuts.

The book she was promoting the day I spent with her during our first meeting in San Francisco was all about life after the Bay Area. We learn, in great detail, about the hot sex she had with Colman Andrews, founder of *Saveur* magazine. Years later, he would end up writing for her at *Gourmet*. She also sketched her adventures at the *Los Angeles Times*, including an episode so painful it always crosses my mind when I see her. She and her husband, television producer Michael Singer, adopted a child whose mother lived in Mexico City and had come to Los Angeles to give the baby away. Just about the time the baby had graduated to eating peas and carrots, the child's mother wanted her back. Ruth and Michael began a prolonged court fight. The issue exploded into a news story portrayed on Spanish-language television as two wealthy American journalists trying to take a baby away from a poor Mexican woman. Finally, they gave Gavi back. By some miracle, Ruth then became pregnant with their son, Nick. The one who hit the Plexiglas in the cab. He's a young man now.

But mostly, the day, like the book, was about food. Glorious, delicious food eaten the way you imagine someone like Ruth Reichl would eat it. That is, with a sense of unhurried purpose and enough knowledge and access to be sampling the best of its class.

"There's still a part of me that disapproves of what I do," she said as we rambled through the big suite during a break in the day.

Not that it was about to stop her. She worked hard for the money that day, smiling at everyone who wanted to talk to her, always compliant with the handlers who set up radio interviews and a lunch and book signings and finally a dinner made from recipes selected from the book and prepared by a team of cooks at a nice French restaurant north of San Francisco. The $95-a-person fee included the meal, wine, an autographed copy of the book and time with the author. It sold out in seconds, of course. But the cooks weren't as smitten as the ticket holders. They thought asparagus dipped in balsamic vinegar, a warm salad with goat cheese, crab cakes and a sweet chocolate cake that one of the chefs derided as "what you serve a child" wasn't sophisticated enough.

Ruth was horrified. She had thought the meal would be served informally at the bookstore. Had she known she would have some of the Bay Area's best French chefs at her disposal, she would have chosen something more elegant.

"I am so sorry," she told them. "I had no idea we would have a real kitchen."

I had a huge amount of sympathy for her at that moment. She made mistakes. She felt vulnerable. She was someone other people made fun of. Maybe we had more in common than I thought. We might be friends, after all. So I asked Ruth how she could have written such personal information. How she could stand exposing herself.

"I think privacy is overrated," she said. "There is no other way I could have written this book except honestly. If you're going to tell stuff, you might as well tell the real stuff."

Except was it all real? Ruth's basic conceit is that her books are true to her life. At least, the spirit of her life. That is, the events happened, mostly, though not exactly as drafted. The dialogue was a work of fiction, but it was true in the sense that the basis for the conversation happened. As she explains it in her book: "In some cases I've exaggerated, in others I've conflated a few meals into one, or combined events that took place over a space of time into a single afternoon or evening."

So there is a fundamental difference, a place where I could begin to see where her approach and mine could be different but that mine was best for me. It would take some time before I would understand this comforting concept: There is more than enough for everybody and comparison only leads to trouble, but I think at that moment I saw a glimmer of that truth.

Toward the end of what had now been more than sixteen hours together, her driver took us back over the Bay Bridge. We talked a little about Marion Cunningham. Turns out that Marion saved her, too. Ruth wasn't a drunk like Marion and me. But like Marion, she was agoraphobic. Marion helped her get over it, and one of the big moments was when Ruth realized, with Marion's help, that she could drive across this very bridge. Then she leaned her head back against the seat, all exhausted and dreamy.

"I never get over the feeling of crossing this bridge," she said. "This feels like home. It really does. There are places you land and it just feels good."

That's how it was for me in California. Despite all the fear and the poor circumstances of my arrival in the Golden State, it immediately felt like home. But it wouldn't be long before I would leave it and head to New York, where I would finally understand the real lesson Ruth had to teach me.

Leaving California for New York was one of the hardest decisions I'd ever made, only slightly worse than having to leave my first big girl crush at Camp Robinwood after possibly the best summer camp experience ever—still miss you, Tex!

Northern California was starting to feel like home. Of course, some of its appeal was situational. For one, I never really had a hometown so there was nothing to compare it to. Plus, after living in Alaska for a long time, the lovely weather and whirl of culture made the Bay Area seem like Shangri-La. But more important, I was, for the first time since I'd been a teenager, seeing the world without the screen of alcohol or drugs. And it was a very, very bright world. Painfully bright, sometimes. But I was experiencing each day completely.

The Bay Area was geographically close to the kind of wild, open space I had grown to love in Alaska, but it was urban enough to keep me from starving for culture. I woke up and learned something new every day. The seasons shifted so often that there was something fresh and seasonal at the farmers' market every couple of weeks. I could begin to fill in the vast holes in my cultural library. My desk at the paper was just around the corner from a new test kitchen, where I learned how to be a better cook. Sometimes, I could smell the recipes the culinary school interns were earnestly cooking even before I got through the door. We had an herb garden on the roof and a 10,000-bottle wine cellar in the basement, which I appreciated for the bragging rights although not the content.

I plowed through each assignment as if it was destined for the front page, which some of them were. I came to understand that you could tell any story, large or small, through food. The space program, the state of the poor and the state of the rich, life as a soldier, life as a star—all of it could be told through the prism of what was on the table, or what wasn't. And I really adored the people I worked with. We had wars and crying fits and shared moments of pure exhilaration. We worked hard, cheered each other on, threatened to quit, gossiped and traveled together. I know I hit a rare level of camaraderie. This was before the *Chronicle*, like newspapers all over the country, imploded along with the economy. Phil Bronstein, who was the executive editor, still spent money on us like a drunken sailor. He trusted Michael Bauer, and liked to show us off. He'd bring by his now ex-wife, the actor Sharon Stone, who spent one office Christmas party playing with my hair and offering to cut it if I came by the house. Later it was actors like Robin Williams and Sean Penn, who once sat in the wine cellar with Phil drinking the best bottle we could find to crack open for them.

My personal life shifted in California, too. I had managed to end with relatively few hysterics a long relationship that I had carried down with me from Alaska. And then I began to see Katia. What a refreshing thing, taking a lover instead of a hostage. This is what talking to other recovering alcoholics on a regular basis and a little therapy can do for a girl.

Katia had been living in New York and reporting for *Newsday*.

She liked her job and she loved New York, but I knew from my long weekends with her that there was no way I was going to abandon the Pacific Ocean and all those Meyer lemons and my crew at the *Chronicle* to live where there was nothing but concrete, graffiti and eight million people who refused to say good morning to each other. So even though I halfheartedly looked for work in New York to make Katia happy, I was hoping for another solution. Mr. Bronstein came to my rescue and hired her to write about City Hall. Katia is the only child of a single mother who had emigrated from Cuba, so the fact that her mother lived a few hours away from San Francisco made the move easier.

But just when I thought I had dodged the New York bullet, I started to circulate more with people from *The New York Times,* most notably Sam Sifton, who would engineer my job there, and the late Johnny Apple, whose nod of approval helped grease the process. I met Johnny when, much to my surprise, I was invited to be on a food and journalism panel at the University of Michigan with him. In classic Apple style, he grabbed hold of the panel. Mimi Sheraton was there, too, as was New York University food professor Marion Nestle and school lunch reformer Ann Cooper, women who would in the years that followed significantly move the national ball forward when it came to how well America eats. But even they just sat there and listened, hoping to wedge in a thought here or there as Johnny's monologue continued.

Finally, I had my shot. It was 2003, the height of the second wave of the Atkins craze. So I made a joke about how Atkins dieters are like the followers of the cult leader Jim Jones, except the Kool-Aid is sugar-free. (OK, for the record Jim Jones made his followers drink cyanide-laced Flavor Aid, but I was making a joke, not a monument to historical accuracy.) Johnny laughed hard, and after the panel he threw an arm around me. He noticed me! This would come in handy later.

Meanwhile, Katia wasn't loving life in San Francisco. She missed New York. She sometimes jokes that there are only eleven other Sephardic Cuban lesbians in the world, and they all live in New York City.

"I need to get back to my people," she told me.

And I was starting to wonder if there was something more out there. Unlike a lot of my more skilled and ambitious colleagues in journalism, I hadn't really imagined working at *The New York Times*. I'm not being modest here. I seriously never felt that I had what it took. It was kind of like playing first base for my women's recreational softball team. I was a star on that team, but that didn't mean I could play for the Yankees. Besides, I loved the *Chronicle*. Given that I had almost lost my career and my life to addiction (and this is no exaggeration), I figured I better hold on to what I had and work on being grateful.

Then I got an e-mail from Sam, who was then the editor of the Dining section and who, after a stop as culture editor, would later become the *Times* restaurant critic.

"Hey, Kim—can you give me a call?"

That was it. The planets had aligned; the perfect job was open writing about food for the *Times*. Did I want to make a run at it? At the end of the day, who doesn't want to play for the Yankees?

So we packed up the Honda CR-V, put Lucy, my sweet old dog, in the backseat and headed across the Bay Bridge. Good-bye, heirloom tomatoes. Good-bye, Pacific Ocean. Good-bye, Meyer lemons.

I arrived in New York just another naive schmuck humming a few lines from "New York, New York." I was terrified and already homesick, but I thought somehow my new life wouldn't be that bad.

Ha ha.

I quickly saw that New York City was extreme in the way Alaska was extreme. Although one was as barren and rural as the other was crowded and urban, they were both wild and impersonal. In either place, make a big enough mistake and you are instantly part of the food chain. A 2009 study from the Pew Research Center measuring where people most want to live showed that 45 percent of Americans between the ages of eighteen and thirty-four wanted to live in New York City. Only 14 percent of people thirty-five and older wanted to live there. Big cities are for the young, and I was not that young anymore.

And perhaps the most sobering (ha!) fact about New York? Besides the people whom I come home to every night, no one would really care if I got swallowed up or not. My disappearance would just mean a little more cheese for the other rats in the race.

Early on, I cut out a *New Yorker* cartoon that still hangs on our refrigerator. Two businessmen are walking through the streets of New York. One is holding his briefcase over his head, protecting himself from a flying pig with fangs.

"That's what I hate about this city," he says. "You roast in the summer, you freeze in the winter, and the rest of the time it's carnivorous pig bats."

To this day, it's the pig bats that get to me.

We settled in Park Slope, Brooklyn, for three main reasons. It was close to a huge park where I could run my dog. We could afford a place with a tiny backyard so I could still pretend I was somewhere not so urban. And there was a big food co-op where I could buy fruit and vegetables from a couple hundred miles away and decent meat from animals that had been raised on pasture. That Katia had lived there before and knew the place well didn't hurt, either. And although at the time having a baby together was merely interesting pillow talk, the fact that it was near one of the few great public elementary schools in New York closed the deal.

After California, the challenge of foraging for food in New York was a shock. The supermarkets were overcrowded and stocked with dusty cans of tomatoes and corned beef hash and plastic bags of Dole produce. They smelled dead. Neighborhood bodegas with decent produce in their bins offered a little relief, but you could never tell where the cucumbers or butter lettuce was from or how long it had been sitting there. Almost every restaurant charged $8 or $10 for salads of soggy mesclun mix that I swore came out of the same huge bag stashed somewhere in the Bronx. I couldn't find a seasonal rhythm in much of the food, save for apples and shad roe and ramps. And I won't even start with the misplaced pride people have in their Jersey tomatoes.

Ruth had grown up here. She loved it. I must be missing something, I thought.

I t was early November 2004 when I went to work at *The New York Times*. I would ride a crowded subway car for forty-five minutes every morning and walk up into Times Square. It was like making my way through a pinball machine. Then, when it was over, I would trudge home through the dark of a New York winter.

At first, all I could see was the grime, the poverty, the gray light that seemed to settle into every corner. I had yet to discover the beauty of the city. I was shocked every day, baffled that people could bump against each other constantly but act as if they were alone on the island. Once I was talking with my mother on my cell phone and stepped into a crosswalk. I had the right of way, the light was green and the little white walking guy was flashing in my favor. The truck driver didn't care. As he blew by me, inches from my face, I instinctively yelled out, "Asshole!"

"What?" my mother said. "Honey, are you mad at me?"

I couldn't stand the smells, the lack of eye contact, the relentless drive to get in front of the person who was in front of you. And what was with all the garbage that piled up on the sidewalks? What was I doing in a city whose government published a map showing where the rats live? The summer turned out to be even worse. We didn't have the money to rent a house on the beach for a week, much less the season. So we were left to explore the nearby beaches on the weekend, sitting in sand filled with cigarette butts and old diapers.

From the first day I walked into the Times building, it became quickly apparent that my soft life as a West Coast food writer was over. There was no test kitchen filled with eager-to-please interns. No herb garden to escape to between deadlines. I barely knew the difference between Joe Torre and Jacques Torres. Not only did I have to learn an entirely new newsroom culture, I had to learn the culinary canon of an entire new coast, from the fish species to the history of the restaurants.

And the sharp elbows were everywhere.

Physically, the Times building on 43rd Street was a dump, a warren of bad office furniture, pasty guys in Dockers and Rockports and carpet so worn you had to look down when you walked or you'd trip. Empty desks were covered in reams of paper and overflowing manila folders and boxes. Occupied desks were even worse. The color was beige accented with gray. Still, it was so cool to be there. This was the place where the best editors in the business decided to publish the Pentagon Papers and where countless other equally important news decisions had been made. For a girl whose first newspaper story was printed before she had her driver's license, it was electric.

An editor showed me my desk and told me to get settled. I put my backpack on the floor, careful so it didn't touch the sticky trap set out for the mice. I tried to start my outdated PC, but the tech people had yet to set it up for a new employee. Later I would learn this was the same desk that Ruth Reichl used to sit at. With not much to do until my computer worked, I took the elevator up to the cafeteria, and detoured into the long hall of Pulitzers. Starting with a Pulitzer from 1918, every one of the one hundred or so pieces of work that won the highest prize in journalism marched across the walls that led to the executive suites. The trophy case at my parents' house flashed in front of my eyes. I had that feeling that had come up so many times before.

I am so over my head, I thought.

When I finally got down to work, the writing didn't come easily. The breezy, straight-ahead writing style that had worked so well at the *Chronicle* was considered sloppy and sophomoric at the *Times*. The funny little asides and goofy structural gimmicks just didn't fly. In the beginning, even the good stuff got killed. It wasn't like anyone was ordering major rewriting. Rather, there were so many editors, each shaving a little here, grinding off a bit there, that it was death by emery board. Explanations were awkwardly thrust into the middle of otherwise perfectly good, short sentences. Contractions were eliminated.

But mostly, I had lost my confidence, and it showed. My editors and friends back in California said I just didn't sound like myself anymore. I had lost my mojo.

It was during this period that I got a couple of good lessons from some of the grand dames of food writing in New York. Like so many freshly minted new arrivals, I was an easy mark.

Florence Fabricant, a legendary food reporter at the *Times*, asked me to lunch.

"The Four Seasons!" she announced.

This would be so cool. I clipped along behind Florence, in her perfect scarf and sensible heels, imagining our grand entrance into the dining room of the Four Seasons, once the temple of high-end power dining, on 52nd Street. Although it has since faded, the concept of seasonality was in full swing there long before California cuisine took hold. Maybe we would get a coveted seat near the famous white marble pool, or a power table in the Grill Room. Me and Florence Fabricant at the legendary Four Seasons! I was the pooh, and everyone else could just take a whiff.

We arrived and were whisked immediately down the hall to the Pool Room. Henry Kissinger, looking small and rumpled, was holding court at a table across the way. We had consommé with foie gras dumplings, and I tasted, for the first time, those tiny Nantucket Bay scallops, each one a little sugar bomb with an overarching whiff of seawater. The marshmallows of the ocean, I once heard them called. I finally understood why. It was the beginning of an entirely new level of benchmarks, East Coast–style.

The check came, and Florence told me to put it on my expense account. I had never really talked to my bosses about the expense account policy. I was so new I had had no occasion to expense anything yet. I expected that basic things I needed to report stories—plane fare, books, certain meals and ingredients to test recipes—would be legitimate. But this lunch? I looked at the bill. It was over $200.

I went back to the office, sheepish. Kathleen McElroy, who had taken over as Dining editor from Sam and was a very kind person, had mercy.

"This time," she said in a way I knew meant it shouldn't happen again. And it didn't, until the following week when Marian Burros stuck me with the bill from our lunch at Esca, which would come to be my favorite expensive seafood restaurant in New York.

Not too much later I had a welcome-to-New-York lunch with Mimi Sheraton at the Gotham Bar and Grill. She put the fear of God into me. No one was going to look out for me at the *Times* but me, she said. I had to be my own brand. (I still have no idea what that means.) And, she said, I should never share a byline, a rule I would break many times.

Then she let me pick up the tab, too.

At the end of the day, I'm a tough kid. Scared out of my mind, but tenacious. So slowly, I started to find my way through the machine that is New York. I got my sea legs at work and started to write stories that felt like me. Once I sorted out the alphabet soup of the subway system, I came to appreciate its democratizing effect. I even learned how to organize my train *mise en place*, figuring exactly which car I needed to board in order to be perfectly placed for a transfer or the right set of exit stairs.

The constant mash-up of cultures and people, all rubbing shoulders, creates a place unlike any other in the world. And I was a part of it. Some days I ended up talking George Foreman grills with Jimmy Breslin in his apartment or eating salami with Frances

McDormand. I could get Jamaican beef patties at two A.M. and warm bagels delivered in the morning. With nothing more than a Metro card and a few dollars, I could get a perfect bowl of pork ramen or a plate of West Indian goat curry or mozzarella so fresh it was still warm. I even had moments when I understood what made New York beautiful. From a friend's rooftop garden, I saw how the city sparkled with promise. I felt the magic quiet of Central Park when it snowed that really big, soft snow. I learned that the proportion of assholes to angels is probably about the same as any other city and that springtime in New York, like springtime everywhere, made everyone happier.

And on the train ride home every night, I could look toward Ellis Island and see the Statue of Liberty and think of my grandmother's journey to America. Florence Ranallo Zappa, my mom's mom, poor and illiterate, had been one of twelve million immigrants to pass through the New York immigration center. Could she have imagined what kind of life her granddaughter would have because of the sacrifices she made?

That helped make up for the days when I felt like I was living like a rat. I still had doubts that I could find my way through the land of raw ambition. Here, in the place where food was often more fashion than dinner, I was a misfit. I would never have the money or the degree or the panache that it takes to really fit in.

But this is where Ruth, my very own personal popular girl, comes in. After my byline showed up in the paper a few times, I reached out to Ruth. Would she like to have lunch?

"I would love to," she wrote me in an e-mail.

She had been meaning to get in touch with me since I landed, she said. Maybe it was one of the polite lies that grease so much of

SPOON FED · *111*

New York life, but I didn't care. We were going to have lunch, and surely Condé Nast would pick up the tab.

Of course, I was out of my mind with nerves. Who wouldn't be? This was the powerful and fabulous Ruth Reichl, the Condé Nast editor who slipped through the city in a black Town Car that was always at her disposal. This was the most famous woman in food writing in America. I had met her before, sure, but this was different. We were going to just be chatting, like friends or colleagues. I couldn't hide behind my notebook.

Ruth liked to hold her lunches at a place called Sushi Zen on 44th Street. It's a precise, delicious sushi restaurant with a kind of impersonal midtown New York feel to it. It was just around the corner from her office, and the owners adored Ruth, of course. So lunch was always whatever the chef felt would please Ms. Reichl.

I had yet to figure out how long it actually takes to walk anywhere in New York, which is a skill that takes some time to acquire. When you're new and someone tells you where to meet them and you look at the map and see it is fifteen blocks away, you have no way to judge how long it will take. Some blocks take seven minutes to get across, others three. There are shortcuts and crowds to account for. So I arrived way too early and stood awkwardly in the lobby, feeling big and hulky and in the way. She finally swept in. We did the stupid double kiss thing, then headed immediately to her table. It's a little two-top to the right of the door but toward the back of the restaurant. Stupidly, I took the booth side. I would later learn that Ruth always sits there.

A woman came to the table.

"Feed us," Ruth said.

In no time, I began babbling. I don't know what I said, but she just seemed to keep beaming up at me with that damn Cheshire cat smile, which only made me tap dance harder. I was drowning before I even got near the water.

We started with mushroom broth, then took in a parade of sushi and sashimi. I continued to babble. She murmured through the mackerel and purred past the tuna belly.

"I always save the uni for last," she said. "It's like dessert."

I nodded, my mouth prematurely full of uni.

I could not tell you what we talked about, except I know it involved the latest we had each heard about Marion Cunningham. Like a pair of siblings, at least we could always talk about Mom.

A few months later, I was starting to feel like New York was not going to swallow me up whole after all. I was still not a part of the city, but living here was starting to feel pretty cool. The landscape was shifting. I had gotten on the front page a couple of times. I didn't drag in the door at the end of each night exhausted from the pace. I was seeing plays and listening to music and eating all kinds of things I had never tasted before. And I was confident enough to e-mail Ruth and boldly suggest another lunch. I had discovered a southern Indian place nearby. Would she want to meet me there?

"There's no Indian place on Forty-sixth," she writes back.

Ha! There is! I actually know something she didn't! It was a feeling not unlike finding out the nasty head cheerleader now weighed three hundred pounds and lived in a trailer.

I meet her in the lobby of Condé Nast and off we went.

Eating at this place was a logistical challenge. You had to make your way to the back of the restaurant and jump on line, trying to scan the specials and peer into the steam table pans so when the time came you'd be ready. A lot of the young Indian office workers in the area made it their regular cafeteria, and they knew exactly what they wanted and were in a hurry to get it. The pressure to order quickly was fierce.

I spotted a rare empty table right by the door and told Ruth to grab it, then I went to the back and ordered a couple of mango lassis and spicy masala dosas, which gave me the starch and spiciness I craved, especially in the New York winter. I made my way back to the table with an orange tray loaded with food. We caught up on Marion Cunningham. We talked a little about the paper and the magazine. Chitchat. We both really dug the food, but as usual, I felt like I was boring the crap out of her. She was still the cool, popular girl, no matter how well I seemed to be doing.

Toward the end of the meal, the office workers thinned out and an old woman lurched in. She had a crumpled brown paper bag that she had fashioned into kind of a bowl. She had on several layers of clothes, and although I can't recall if this is true or just my mind filling in the details, she smelled strongly of old cigarettes and boiled urine. I tensed up and prepared my New York face. My plan was to act cool and ignore her until she went away or became someone else's problem. I might even call the manager over if I had to.

Ruth took out a five-dollar bill and put it in her bag. She smiled at the woman until a worker at the restaurant hurried over and sent her out the door.

"I always give money to women on the street," Ruth said.

She took a last bite of dosa.

"What if that was my mother and no one would give her a thing?"

At that moment, a couple of things occurred to me. First, the only way to survive New York was to have a good set of guidelines. Ruth's rule of always giving money to women on the street is one. There are many others, which I picked up from all the people who were kind to me when I first moved to New York: Never take a taxi during rush hour because the subway will always be faster. Never get out of a cab on the left and always tell the cab driver you are going from Manhattan to Brooklyn *after* you get in the car. Always go to the bathroom when you have a chance even if you don't think you have to. Never stop in the middle of the sidewalk to make a call or look up directions.

My dear friend and fellow food writer Julia Moskin is a lifelong New Yorker who stepped right in and scooped me up when I arrived at the *Times.* She taught me a lot. She showed me how to navigate the little food shops in Queens and Brooklyn. She explained that those candied peanuts and cashews sold from the street carts never live up to their promise, but that dirty water hot dogs usually do. She had us over for our baby's first Passover and she taught me that the time, cost and headaches involved in a trip to the airport always outweigh the impulse to be a good host and pick someone up. (I make an exception for my parents, and for young relatives who have never been to New York before. But even those exceptions earn me eye rolls from Julia.)

But the ultimate lesson from that period in my life came, like a beautiful gift, at yet another lunch with Ruth. This time, instead of the busy Indian place, she suggested we go back to her favorite sushi restaurant. I had an agenda. I wanted to tell her about this book, and about how I wanted to write about women cooks who taught me life lessons. I confessed everything, the need I had for role models in the kitchen and at the computer, about my early obsession with her and my constant feeling that she was so much cooler than I could ever hope to be.

She laughed. It seemed like she laughed for a long time.

"That's funny," she said. "I always felt that way about Alice. I was like the Little Match Girl pressing my face against the window, especially in Berkeley. Everyone was having better parties, doing better drugs, having better sex."

She saw her books as studies in insecurity, about never measuring up. I never read them like that. I saw a self-satisfied woman with a passel of exquisite food and sexual experiences I could never have and a better writer than I could ever hope to be.

My popular girl, insecure?

Then Ruth took my hands, looked into my eyes, and told me I was actually her hero, that she always looked up to me. That I was the kind of writer she could only hope to be. She said I could use her Town Car whenever I wanted, and when I was ready I could become the editor in chief of *Gourmet* and even move into her apartment.

OK, I made up that last paragraph.

But here is the truth I learned from Ruth: Popular girls are my own boogeymen, made of my own free will. Because I worried I might never be good enough, I couldn't stop comparing myself— especially to women who rightly should be my best allies.

What a waste of time, all that measuring myself against other people. The only ruler that matters is the one I pull out at the end of the day. Did I do my best? Did I tell the truth? Was I helpful to my fellows?

And, did I make something good to eat?

I am offering you a recipe from Ruth called Matzo Brei. I like to call it Popular Girl Breakfast.

The dish is brilliant in its simplicity. It's nothing more than butter, matzo crackers and eggs all in a scramble. As Ruth says in the intro to the recipe in the *Gourmet* cookbook, the secret is butter and lots of it.

It is the only thing her mother taught her to cook. She used to make it for her drunken high school friends, when she wanted to feel popular. "I wasn't a cheerleader or a dancer and nobody ever asked me to the drive-in," she once wrote. But she could cook. Like me, she figured out early that cooking can make you feel like less of an outcast.

With a recipe for Popular Girl Breakfast in your back pocket, you'll never have to climb into the bottom of your sleeping bag again.

MATZO BREI

4 matzos
4 large eggs
1 teaspoon salt
6 tablespoons (¾ stick) unsalted butter

1. Crumble matzos into a large sieve placed over a bowl to catch crumbs; then hold sieve under cold running water until matzos are moist and softened but not completely disintegrated, about 15 seconds.

2. Transfer to the bowl with crumbs, add eggs and salt, and mix lightly with a fork.

3. Heat butter in a 10- or 12-inch skillet over moderate-high heat until foam subsides. Add matzo mixture and cook, stirring constantly, until eggs are scrambled and matzo has begun to crisp, about 3 minutes.

NOTE: I find a few grinds of black pepper at the table help with the character of this dish.

Yield: *4 servings*

5

I'll Take Another Meatball

My Italian is so bad I have a hard time pronouncing *gnocchi*, but I grew up hearing enough of the language to know when I'm being yelled at. And that's definitely what was happening at a table in a small roadside restaurant in Abruzzi.

I had driven through the Italian mountains with an interpreter to find Ateleta, the village where my grandmother Florence Ranallo Zappa grew up. I had come in search of a recipe. But really, I had come to search for some clues. Anyone examining his or her relationship with food has to start at the beginning. That is, with the people who fed us first. So to finally understand why the kitchen would come to save me—and maybe why I needed to be saved in the first place—I had to understand why my mother cooks the way she does. And to do that, I had to go to where her mother was born and figure out why she cooked the way she did. Fortunately, that was Italy.

It took me long enough to get there. Every time I got even a little close to making the trip happen, I'd get distracted. Work schedules got in the way, or I got entwined in some sort of financial or emotional drama that kept the dream tamped down. Then there was the part where I never had much money (see previous sections on small newspapers) and I wasn't all that great at saving what I did have (see previous sections on drug and alcohol use).

Sometimes, other trips just seemed to matter more. I had lived most of my adult life in the West. That made parts of Asia and Russia closer. One year I took classes at Le Cordon Bleu in Paris designed for candy-assed tourists such as myself. Another I toured Turkey with my brother, the art expert, and my parents. I made it to the Russian Far East for work and to Vietnam with my best friend. But no matter how many stamps I crammed into my passport, Italy always remained the nagging and embarrassing exception. What kind of food writer hasn't been to Italy? And, older Italians especially liked to ask, what kind of Italian-American girl hasn't found time to visit home?

Back when I was working for the *Chronicle*, I was finally ready to take the trip. I was at the airport with a ticket in my hand. My mother, my brother and an aunt were going to meet me there and we would all go to the village together to celebrate my fortieth birthday, which was the next day, September 12, 2001.

The first clue something was wrong came when we were in line to check in. Our flight was canceled. The ticket agent couldn't tell us why. But if we all just stayed where we were, someone would be back soon to rebook us. Then all the television screens went blank. A traveler in line behind me said there had been a plane crash in New York. I jumped out of the line and called the city desk.

"The United States is under attack," I recall an editor telling me. None of the paper's reporters could get into the airport. I was to stay there and try to interview family members who had people on United Flight 93. It had taken off from Newark and was headed to

San Francisco when the terrorists hijacked it. It crashed in a Pennsylvania field.

"But I'm the food writer," I remember saying to myself as I hung up with the city desk.

Five years later, having made the move to New York and settled down with Katia, I decided, once again, that it was time. Barring another major disaster, nothing was going to stop me. I had to get to the village where my grandmother was born. I needed to track the path that began there and ended with the pot of red sauce that simmers on my stove on Sunday afternoons. I hoped that when I found that recipe, I would finally understand who I was, and why the kitchen was the only room in the house that really matters to me.

Maybe I'm hungry to figure out where I'm from because I don't really have an official hometown. People ask me where I'm from and I can't answer them. My dad's company sent us from Wisconsin to California to Michigan to Texas and then back to Michigan, where I finally got off the family train and went to college. Through it all, the one constant was my mother's spaghetti sauce. As soon as we got the kitchen shelf paper laid and she figured out where the grocery store was, she made the sauce. It meant this was home, and that first plate of spaghetti and meatballs made us all feel as if everything was going to be OK. Now, with several more states' worth of my own transfers behind me, the first thing I cook in a new kitchen is a big pot of sauce. When my siblings and I visit each other, spaghetti is on the menu.

But once I got to the village where it all supposedly began, things didn't go so great. At a table covered with oilcloth in the little dining room of La Bottega dell'Arte Salata, the small rosticceria a distant cousin owns in a town called Castel de Sangra, I sat down with the closest relative I could find, Filomena Sciullo Ranallo. She was my grandmother's sister-in-law.

As far as I could tell, the dozen people who came by the restaurant to meet me were thrilled one of the American relatives came to visit. They explained with great pride how Madonna had tried to find her relatives at a nearby village a few years ago and failed. But not you, they told me. You are luckier than Madonna.

They grilled lamb chops and set out platters of tomatoes. We ate some flat pasta with a simple tomato sauce, and then I got down to business. I pulled out a notebook and my camera and set about recording what I could about how everyone in the room cooked. I was trying to write down the recipe for the sauce we had just eaten when the old woman grabbed my arm, shaking it hard. Why didn't I speak any Italian? And even worse, why did I think oregano had any place in tomato sauce?

Well, because my mother put oregano in her sauce. But oregano, like the meatballs I add to the pot, was only one of the twists and turns the recipe had taken during nearly a century in America. It turns out that there is no single iconic red sauce in my grandmother's village. There are sauces with lamb, an animal the village organizes an entire festival around. There are sauces with only tomato and basil, sauces just for lasagna and sauces just for grilled meats. Small meatballs might go in a broth, but never in sauce for pasta. In fact, only two things in the village reminded me of anything I grew up with. The fat pork sausages were cooked and served the same way, and my Italian cousins looked just like my brothers.

To understand why I made my sauce the way I did, I needed to start closer to home, with my mother. She has been making spaghetti sauce for almost sixty years, from a recipe she learned from her mother, who had made it with American ingredients since the early 1900s. My grandmother had been shipped to America, literally and largely against her will, to marry an Italian named John Zappa. They raised eleven children. My mother, Anne Marie, was the second youngest.

John Zappa ran a relatively big dairy farm in a very little town called Cumberland in northwest Wisconsin. He was, by all accounts, a tough farmer with a mean streak who built a name for himself among the immigrants in the area. He amassed enough land that some of it is still being farmed by my uncles and cousins.

He died before I was born. My grandparents had just moved from the big farm house to a smaller place nearby where Grandpa could still keep a garden and a few farm animals. He had walked out of the house to feed them when the heart attack hit. Grandma Zaps looked out the window and saw him on the ground, his body on top of the bundle of oats he had been carrying. She was illiterate, even in Italian, and she didn't know how to dial the phone to call for help.

To the day she died, which was many years later, Grandma Zaps spoke only enough English to communicate the most basic things to her dozens of bored American grandchildren, of whom I was one.

My mother's family could not be more different from my father's. James Howard Severson is a hard-headed Norski through and through. His people are Norwegian, with a little Irish and English from his mother's side. His side of the family was circumspect, controlled and often nonemotive. My mother's was all loud and emotional and filled with food and guilt. Growing up, depending on who was mad at me, I was either getting yelled at or no one was talking to me.

My dad is a former nationally ranked ski jumper and an outdoorsman of the first order. He is a hunter, and I can't remember a fall when he didn't give me packages of deer or elk wrapped in white paper from the custom butcher. He's a straight arrow, my dad, who believes in working hard, finishing what you start, the Republican Party and the spiritual value of a day in the woods. But he also likes a party, a drink, a joke and a roomful of people. Like my mother, he grew up without much extra money around.

"Didn't even have enough money for Novocain," he told me once. The story is pretty horrific. He was a young boy with thirteen cavities. His father told the dentist to just go ahead and fill them, but to not use any of the costly extra medicine. My dad just held tight to the arms of the dentist chair, trying not to cry or breathe in the smoke from the drill on his teeth.

"Tough little bugger, aren't you," he remembers the dentist saying.

Culturally, I veer toward the Zappa side (except maybe the hardheaded part, which is all Severson). Even in high school, I thought being Italian was the coolest thing. For a time, I got great pleasure from imagining that my mother's family had loose ties to the Mafia. In high school, I lied and told my pals that Frank Zappa was my cousin. But the overarching reason I grew up feeling mostly Italian was the food. When I looked at the food of their respective cultures and realized the choice basically came down to lutefisk or Italian sausage, I leaned toward the Italians. And you don't need a psychology degree to figure out that the food my mother cooked was tied directly to the emotional center of our house. Although they accept or reject it in their own way, my brothers and sister are linked deeply to the kitchen because of my mother, who made sure her children kept coming back to her by cooking for them.

Even my dad, who fights to keep the Norwegian alive and still likes a meat sandwich and a good, simple bowl of bean soup, admits the food my mother brought to the relationship was far superior to the boiled dinners of his youth. Back in the 1930s and '40s, in the part of Wisconsin my dad grew up in, Italians and their food were still strange, foreign and low in the social order. His mother so hated that her blue-eyed baby boy was dating an Italian that she threatened to boycott the wedding.

Before he met my mother, the only Italian food my father had tasted was pasta from a can or the food served to him when he babysat for some people he vaguely describes as "the Italian family who lived by the ski jump." But he remembers clear as a bell the first time he ate spaghetti and Italian sausage—what he calls "the good stuff"—when he traveled north to visit my mother's family on the farm in Cumberland.

"I was somewhat apprehensive going up there with all the Italians around and not being totally familiar with it," he said. "But this was the routine thing for them, this big meal and the platters full of spaghetti and sausage and the wine and what have you. None of the women sat at the table. They served, which was totally unusual for me. I thought, *That's not good.*"

My grandmother put on spreads like that every Sunday, with help from her daughters.

"We always had a pot of spaghetti sauce and meatballs ready," my mom said. "Before we would go to church, Mother would put a whole chicken in the oven, and when we'd get back it was done."

My mom's siblings were always hungry right after mass at St. Anthony's, the church in Wisconsin she grew up in. To keep them at bay until the main meal was ready, my grandmother made them sauce sandwiches. (A sauce sandwich is just what it sounds like: a piece of bread—slightly soft Italian bread is best—on a plate with sauce spooned over it. For people really in a hurry, the bread may be dipped directly into the pot.) The spaghetti would go on the table along with the chicken and the meatballs and a plate of Italian sausage and prosciutto my grandfather had cured himself. You can see why a plate of fish cured in lye might not compare.

Among my four siblings and me, how Mom makes her sauce has been a constant source of discussion. We're all good cooks, some much better than others. Still, none of us can get it just right. But we try, then we talk about it with each other and try some more. When does she put in the paste? Is a little bit of roasted pepper essential? Do you need to use oregano in the meatballs?

This is a problem my cousins have, too. Sharon Herman still lives in Cumberland, not far from the Zappa family dairy farm. Her mother (my aunt and godmother, the late Phillomena DeGidio) was one of the oldest of the eleven Zappa kids. She has long been considered the best sauce maker. My father can still catalog the distinct tastes of almost every Zappa sister's sauce. Some use loose sausage meat and others are heavy on the peppers. But none compare to Auntie Phil's, which everyone seems to agree is the most like Grandma Zaps's.

"Your father says mine never tastes like Phil's," my mom says. But, she adds with some pride, it's as close as any of her sisters ever got. It's worse for my cousin Sharon, who has lived for years under the cloud of never having mastered the master's sauce.

"I could never figure it out," she told me. "I even took her little hand once and made her measure out all the spices like she did and put them in measuring spoons to try to get the exact amounts. It still didn't taste right."

All the Italian ladies in Cumberland used to put up their own tomatoes, which might be part of the secret. Or perhaps it was the mixture of canned carrots, a couple of celery stalks and the onion and garlic, all pulsed together in the blender, that my aunt used to build the underpinnings of the sauce. My mother doesn't do this, and she never canned her own tomatoes. The master also put in the tomato paste at the end. My mother prefers to first brown the meatballs and pork ribs (a chop will do if you have it) and then deglaze the pan with the paste.

"If you're making it with chuck roast, that's good, too," she said, confusing things even more.

I understand my cousin's frustration. Getting a recipe out of my own mother is like trying to get a four-year-old to explain what happened at day care. She's not one of those annoying and cagey matrons of the kitchen who build their power by dangling the promise of a secret ingredient that will never be revealed. She just cooks by hand, so she's never really able to articulate every step. She can tell you to make sure the meatballs are well browned. ("Don't put those white meatballs into that sauce!" she'll warn.) And she can give you tips on the all-important step called "fixing the sauce"—tasting it toward the end and adding a little red wine vinegar or maybe, in a pinch, a handful of Parmesan cheese to smooth out the flavor. But an exact recipe? Not so much. For example, thin-skinned Italian peppers were always around the farmhouse she grew up in, so she likes to use some kind of pepper to give the sauce what she calls "homemade flavor." She often just uses pickled pepperoncini from a jar, which I do, too. Once, when I was out of them, I called to see if she had a substitute. She suggested green bell peppers.

"But I never put in green peppers," I told her.

"Well, if you had one you would," she said. "But don't go out of your way. It doesn't make that much difference."

OK, Mom. Let's focus.

"When do you put the chicken thighs in?" I asked another time.

"Oh, honey, I never use chicken thighs."

"But last time I was home, the sauce had chicken thighs."

"Huh—that's funny," she said. "I guess I must have had some in the freezer."

These are maddening conversations, but I think they will go on until the day she makes her last pot.

If anything, her sauce, like her mother's sauce, and the sauces from the home village of Ateleta, are about making do. Well-browned meat is the key, but you use the meat you have. In the poor village where my grandmother grew up, meat was a luxury, a flavoring. The sauce was sometimes a way to stretch things out.

I called Arthur Schwartz, the Jewish and Italian food expert who lives not too far from me in Brooklyn. I was hoping he could help me unravel how my meaty family sauce came to be.

"Your ancestors made it with all these bones because that's what they had," he said. Once my grandmother arrived in America, there was plenty of meat around. So the theory is that her sauce graduated from sauce flavored with a bony piece of meat or two from one animal to a full, rich American ragù built from the fat-rich meat of two or three animals. But for her, the sauce was still a way to find a use for the extra parts. On the farm where my mother was born, the men would butcher hogs and fatten up a few of the dairy cows for the family table. So the sauce often simmered with a meaty piece of pork neck bone or a tail or even a steak from a shoulder blade.

My mother, who lived through elementary school without a refrigerator, was often dispatched to the cellar to scrape two or three inches of sealing grease off the top of a crock and return to the kitchen with preserved sausages and pork ribs for the sauce. They still had lots of grease clinging to them, and to this day if my sauce doesn't have a nice sheen of fat on the top it's just no good.

Although it all seems very romantic to me now, my mom happily left the farm to try her hand at beauty school, moving to Eau Claire, Wisconsin, where she found my father at a diner they had all gone to after a dance. His date had spent most of the evening in the bathroom with her friends. My mom didn't.

"And I liked the look of her," he told me.

Like many women who were being trained to be modern American housewives, she was delighted to make him a home using all the modern amenities. As he moved her around the country and they moved a few pegs up the middle-class ladder, she fell in love with convenience foods and the big, clean supermarkets of the suburbs. Unlike her mother, she didn't have to can tomatoes or dry her basil and parsley on cookie sheets. And all the meat came on those nice, clean foam trays. Mom even took to using something food manufacturers call "Italian seasoning" in her sauce. But she'll also use a mix of about three parts dried basil to one part dried oregano.

"I don't always use the dried. It just depends on what's there," she said. "But I figure it's got more taste per teaspoon with the dried." She's so fond of that combination that she'll use it in a lot of dishes. My dad has a special name for her chili: Italian soup.

In Italy, it is rare to find more than one herb flavoring a dish.

My grandmother used parsley and basil, maybe as another one of those American abundance adaptations. But what about the oregano? It is an herb much more common in lower elevations and in Sicily than in the part of Italy my people come from. So why does my mother use it when my grandmother never did?

"I don't know," she said. "I just always put it in there." All the Zappa sisters do.

Still stumped about why the family sauce ended up heavy with oregano and meat, I called Lidia Bastianich, the New York chef who has written much about the transfer of Italian food to America.

"This is a cuisine of adaptation, of nostalgia, of comfort," she said. By overemphasizing some of the seasonings Italian immigrants brought from home, they could more easily conjure it up. Maybe someone from a different part of Italy had brought over oregano and married into the Zappa side, changing the sauce. Maybe it just seemed like a really Italian flavor to the first generation. However the oregano ended up there, it serves as an amplification of home. It makes sure one culture gets heard over the din of another. It's like makeup on an opera singer, exaggerated to make a point and heavy enough to carry to the back row.

Sometimes the adaptations were simply practical. Using tomato paste, for example, was a way to make the watery tomatoes in the United States taste more like the thick-fleshed kind that grew in Italy. Then there is the question of all that meat and the way it's presented at the table. In Italy, pasta and meat are usually separate courses. My family's serving style is to pile the pork and beef and meatballs onto a big platter of spaghetti, sometimes with sausage. That mountain of meat might be an homage to my grandmother, for whom an abundant supply of meat was probably one of the few things she liked about her life in America.

SPOON FED · 131

Or maybe she was just overwhelmed: on a farm with no refrigerator, not a lot of money and eleven children, she didn't have time
for a separate meat and pasta course. She didn't speak enough English and I don't speak enough Italian. And she died before I knew
enough to even ask her these kinds of things.

As hard as my mother tried to get off the farm, I am trying just
as hard to get back. Like her, I use spareribs and a nice, fatty piece
of beef. I try to buy them from local farmers who raise their animals
outdoors on pastures and sell them for prices that make my mother
shake her head. I would give anything to have a crock of sausage
under a layer of pork fat in the cellar. I use fresh basil and fresh
breadcrumbs instead of Progresso in my meatballs, but I still stick
to dried basil and oregano in the sauce. My canned tomatoes come
from Italy, even though my mother thinks Contadina or Hunt's is
just fine.

My sauce never tastes just like hers, but I keep trying. And maybe
that's the problem. Perhaps I'm too fixated on my fancy-pants ingredients. Or perhaps it's just a psychological quirk of the kitchen. The
one that makes you think nothing you cook ever tastes as good as
your mother's.

Around Thanksgiving a few years ago, my parents moved into a
small condominium closer to the center of the small Colorado ski
town they live in. To make room, they were going to sell the family
dining-room table and the old oak kitchen table, which had long
since been stripped of its black paint. Instead, I arranged to have
them shipped east. My brother took the kitchen table, and I called
dibs on the dining-room table. It's a little too big for my Brooklyn
brownstone, and it's not an antique or even an heirloom. My
mother bought it during one of our many transfers simply because
she needed a bigger table. But it's is the dining-room table I grew

up with. The place where the special meals were served. I have eaten hundreds of plates of spaghetti on it. I feel the need to keep it, to pass it on to my children. I want to say, "This was your grandmother's table." I want them to know what I learned when I went home. That we are a people who can always make do, no matter what. And that you can never really know who you are until you know where you came from.

And then I will make them sit down and eat spaghetti, and tell them the story of the red sauce trail.

———

This is a version of my mother's sauce that first appeared in the Dining section of *The New York Times*. Trying to make a recipe like the family spaghetti sauce clean and precise enough for the *Times* standards was a chore. Even now, I encourage you to approach this only as a guideline. This sauce is best when the cook uses a little heart and intuition. It is not so much the amalgam of tomato and pork that makes this sauce good; it is sitting down regularly at the family table to eat it.

SPAGHETTI AND MEATBALLS

THE MEATBALLS

2 pounds ground beef

1 cup fresh breadcrumbs made from two or three slices of dense, coarse bread, crusts removed

½ cup finely grated Parmesan cheese

1 heaping tablespoon fresh chopped basil

1 heaping tablespoon fresh chopped flat-leaf parsley

1 teaspoon kosher salt

½ teaspoon black pepper

⅛ teaspoon ground cayenne pepper

2 cloves garlic, minced

2 eggs

2 tablespoons olive oil

1. Mix all ingredients except olive oil by hand in a large bowl, using a light touch.
2. Take about 2½ ounces of meat in hand and roll between palms to form a ball that is firmly packed but not compressed. Each should be about 2 inches wide—bigger than a golf ball but smaller than a tennis ball.
3. Heat the olive oil over medium-high heat in a large, heavy pot that will later be used for the sauce. When it shimmers, add the meatballs in batches. Don't crowd the meatballs. Allow them to brown well on the bottoms before turning or meatballs will break apart.
4. Continue cooking until browned all over. Don't overcook. Remove them to a plate as each batch is finished.
5. Allow meatballs to cool slightly. Cover and refrigerate until sauce is ready.

Yield: *About 16 meatballs. Recipe can be halved.*

THE SAUCE

Salt and pepper

1 pound pork spareribs, neck bone or pork chop

1 pound chuck roast, blade steak or brisket

1 medium onion, chopped small, about ¾ cup

2 cloves garlic, minced

1 6-ounce can tomato paste

1 teaspoon dried oregano

1 tablespoon dried basil

1 teaspoon dried red pepper flakes

2 teaspoons kosher salt

1 bay leaf

1 can crushed tomatoes (28 ounces), Italian if possible

1 can tomato sauce (28 ounces) or 1 carton of Pomi strained tomatoes
    (26 ounces)

½ teaspoon sugar

2 tablespoons fresh flat-leaf parsley, roughly chopped

4 small or 2 large jarred pepperoncini

1 pound spaghetti

1. Sprinkle salt and pepper all over the pork and beef.
2. Using the same pot and remaining fat from cooking the meatballs, brown the meat quickly and remove.
3. Turning heat to medium, add the onions and cook 3 minutes, stirring.
4. Add the garlic and cook another 3 minutes.
5. Add tomato paste and stir, cooking the paste for a couple of minutes until it absorbs the fat and deglazes the pan.
6. Add the oregano, basil, red pepper, 2 teaspoons salt and bay leaf, stirring to combine.
7. Add the cans of tomatoes and sauce, then fill each can with water and add to the sauce.

8. Stir in sugar, parsley and pepperoncini, add back the two meats and any accumulated juices, and bring sauce to a gentle boil.

9. Turn heat down to a simmer, partially cover and leave the sauce to simmer for two and a half hours or more, stirring regularly.

10. About 20 minutes before serving, add back meatballs and allow them to heat through.

11. To serve, boil 1 pound of spaghetti according to package directions. Drain pan, add spaghetti back to pan and add three cups of sauce, or enough so all the spaghetti is generously coated.

12. Toss pasta in the hot pan for a minute, then put the pasta on a large platter. Pour 2 more cups of sauce over the pasta, then arrange meat and two meatballs per person.

13. Serve with a bowl of sauce and a bowl of Parmesan cheese to pass.

NOTE: Remaining sauce and meatballs can be frozen.

Yield: *6 to 8 servings*

6

God Loves You and You Can't
Do a Thing About It

There are several ways to skip church and still get credit for it. Maybe not credit with God, but that's not the higher power that counted when I was a teenager.

I was raised Catholic, with catechism classes and mass on Sunday and a confirmation name (Frances). I joined the folk mass and learned to work the E-minor chord like the Singing Nun. I even had a short stint answering phones at a convent. Nuns generally don't get a lot of calls, so it was a job I could handle.

"It's volunteer work," my mother said. But I think she secretly hoped the nun thing might take.

I also learned ways to get around attending mass. Usually, we went as a family, but when I was in high school my mom let me go on my own. Big mistake. That's when I figured out how to shave a little time off the hour or so it takes to sit through a Catholic service. About ten minutes before the end, when you shuffle up to the front of the church to take communion, you pretend you're walking back to your seat. But you just keep going until you hit the parking lot.

Skipping out on even a little bit of mass is a dangerous business to get into, and not just because of the potential impact on one's afterlife. You get desensitized and begin to take bigger risks. It's like cheating on a diet. A few extra French fries seem like no big deal at lunch. Then you have a cookie in the afternoon, figuring the day is already shot with the French fries. By dinner, all bets are off. The night ends with you, a chocolate cake and a fork. In the same way, one day you're leaving mass early, the next you're swinging by just to pick up the weekly bulletin of church news so your mom thinks you went. Before you know it, you're taking your little brother for cover, swearing him to secrecy as you chill out for an hour at the local omelet place.

All of this sounds like I didn't really care about God or religion or the state of my soul. But I did. I had just lost focus. I was starting to drink with more regularity. I would steal a little liquor from my parents' collection, or one of my cuter friends would talk an older guy into buying some beer. The next logical step was pot, which I happily smoked when I should have been eating lunch at school or making pompoms for the homecoming float (which, by the way, the proud class of 1979 decided should be a big beer mug and a giant can of Stroh's beer. Did I stand a chance?).

I don't want you to think I was a total wreck. I played softball and volleyball and basketball, even getting varsity letters. My parents were duly concerned when my grades bobbed up and down, but they could always take comfort in the fact that I was at least showing up to work on the high school newspaper, *The Tower*. But you can see the duality that was happening. Partying hard whenever I could get away with it, but holding on as best I could to what I thought I should be doing. Complicating matters was the growing suspicion that I was gay.

The feelings became overwhelming when my parents sent me to journalism camp at Ball State University. I was fifteen, and Cindy was sixteen. We fell instantly in love, although neither one of us had any idea that's what it was. We just liked each other so so so so so very much. We wrote newspaper stories, we partied and we sobbed when camp was over and we had to go back to our different worlds. She lived in Wyandotte. I lived in Grosse Pointe. It was like a lesbian *West Side Story* without the fighting. We were separated by distance and class and the fact that I couldn't yet drive. But Cindy did have a license. So one weekend a few months after our tearful parting at journalism camp, my parents let me invite her over for the weekend. It was great. We hung out with my friends a little, but mostly we talked. About everything. Finally, someone who understood me! On Sunday, she got in her car to leave. She was idling in our circular driveway, her window rolled down and me standing at the door. We kept talking, until I finally leaned in and kissed her. As I pulled my head out of the car, I hit it on the doorjamb. The whole thing was thrilling and awkward and life-changing.

"Bye-bye," she said, and drove off. We would later live together in college, each other's first love until the inevitable need to explore other relationships took over.

Anyway, you can see what a tortuous and exhausting life I was living as a teenager. Jock and journalism geek by day, budding alcoholic gay girl by night. Skipping church just fit in, somehow. It's not like the church had a lot of programming for gay youth. Still, I always had a belief in something bigger than myself. I just never figured I was worthy. Or, maybe, I just couldn't be bothered. Once, when I was nearly thirty, I walked out on the deck of my parents' house in the Rocky Mountains to smoke a cigarette with my dad, back when we both smoked. I asked him, the man raised by a

Holy Roller of a mother but himself a sporadic churchgoer until late in life, if he believed in God.

"Well," he said, looking out over a slice of the Yampa Valley, "the sun comes up and goes down every day, and the seasons change the same way every year. Something has to be responsible for that."

It was about the best explanation I have ever heard. I only wish he had told me that when I was a tortured sixteen-year-old, crashing his car and skipping school and yelling regrettable things at my mother. But even if he had (and who knows, he may well have), I never would have been able to hear the message or take any comfort from it. I was too young.

I did believe in something back then; I just didn't know what or how much. The pull was strong enough that one day I waved down the born-again van that the Jesus enthusiasts drove around near our high school. I climbed in and started to listen to the testimony of the people inside. I pressed my knees into the shag carpet, bowed my head and waited for something to happen. A young man knelt with me, holding my hands. We almost lost our balance each time the van turned a corner. He said a prayer that sounded like this: "Lord Jesus Christ, please come into Kim's heart and take her into your flock. We ask this in Your name."

I kept my eyes closed. I waited. Would the Shepherd come to take me home? Nothing happened. I acted saved anyway. I mean, they had spent all this time on me, and even gave me a ride home. What kind of rude loser would I be if I hopped out of the van unsaved?

Fast-forward with me twenty years or so. I am at a turning point. Either I can stop drinking or I can continue drinking and lose my job, my relationship and, probably by my own hand, my life. I don't mean to sound dramatic but things had gotten that bad. It was my great good fortune that I became friends with a woman who knew how to walk the earth without a big cushion of alcohol.

"Pray," she said.

"To who?" I asked.

"Doesn't matter," my new friend said. "Just pick something. The sun. A doorknob. Whatever you want."

I remember the day clear as a photograph. And I can't explain to you how this worked, but maybe I had just been through enough. I sat on the thick carpet in our cozy little rented house in Anchorage. I looked up and simply asked for help. Cold, pure Alaska light streamed in through a window. At that moment, I understood with great clarity that something—call it whatever you want—had been with me my whole life and was more than happy to keep watching over me. I had found the beginnings of a faith that worked for me, but I was still unsure about it. I didn't realize how deep it went, or whether I could really rely on it, until I met an extraordinary cook in New Orleans named Leah Chase.

Mrs. Chase is famous, in no small part because of her gumbo. But there is something else about her. She knows how to make community, and she has the kind of faith I want. That is, faith that's as tempered as steel and is nothing to be ashamed about.

I met her because Hurricane Katrina nearly wiped out her restaurant, Dooky Chase. In case you don't remember, Hurricane Katrina sent so much water pushing against the poorly constructed, 350-mile federal levee system that significant pieces failed, flooding 80 percent of the city of New Orleans. In all, more than 1,800 people died. Like everyone else in the country with a television, I watched bodies floating in the streets. Poor people on rooftops and in the Superdome begged news crews for help that was slow to come.

The New York Times already had swarms of reporters and photographers rotating in and out of Louisiana, but I thought the paper also needed a food writer there. I wanted to take an inventory of what had happened to the city's 3,400 restaurants, Leah Chase's among them. New Orleans is nothing if not a city built on its stomach. No other place in America has such a compact, discrete food culture nor is as deeply defined by how its people eat. The heart of its food is an amalgam of cultures—indigenous, African and European—but its culinary traditions are set and largely unchangeable. It's a city that protects its food traditions. There is a respect for what has come before that is unmatched in any other city in the United States. Since food and music are what made New Orleans, those would be the things that brought it back.

Few people know more about New Orleans food than Mrs. Chase. She's in her eighties now and has been given almost every culinary award this country can bestow. The big-name chefs all respect her. After all, she is the best Creole cook in America, rightly famous for fried chicken and red beans and rice and a thousand other dishes she has been making since she was a young woman. Using her food as a jumping-off place, Mrs. Chase spent a lifetime lifting up her community. Like my mother, she came from a family with eleven children where food was at the center. And like my mother, she is a dedicated Catholic and a woman of great faith. She learned early on a basic formula that she would come to rely on in even the most trying of situations. Every day, without fail and no matter how bad her circumstances, no matter if a child has died or flood water churned through her livelihood, she does three things:

"First, you pray," she told me. "Then you work. And do for others. That's it."

It sounds easy. But it's not. Faith like that only counts when it's tested. That's when you find out if you really believe.

When she was still Leah Lange, a young woman who had grown up hunting and fishing in a segregated southern Louisiana town, she left home and headed to the French Quarter. She figured she could make a living waiting tables and doing a little cooking. She also met a young trumpet player named Edgar "Dooky" Chase II, who ran his own orchestra. After dating for just a few months, they got married and started a family, which would eventually grow to four children. She was so strict with them that they still raise their eyebrows and shake their heads when you ask them about her style of discipline.

Her in-laws needed help running the family restaurant, which wasn't much more than a po' boy stand in a part of New Orleans called the Treme (say Truh-MAY). It's the neighborhood where jazz was born, and where free people of color first started families and businesses before segregationist laws came along. So Leah started cooking, even though she didn't really know what she was doing. It wasn't all that hard to figure out, she said.

"You look at what other chefs do and you learn from them. You read a lot of books," she said when I asked her how she learned. "I read a lot of books. I still do. I still like to see what other people can do with food."

Although the cooking went well, the relationship with Dooky didn't. They were famous for their disagreements. Maybe he never really got over having to give up the music, and people say that Mrs.

Chase never got over her own disappointment with the man he became. Although she would often threaten to leave, she stayed with him for so many decades because that's what a woman of her generation and her convictions and her faith does. And she always had the people who were hungry for her food to fall back on.

The restaurant became a second living room for black New Orleans. Mrs. Chase made sure of that, because she got her fuel from other people. She made sure the restaurant was always full and wove into it her love of baseball, politics, music and art. Mrs. Chase, who still wears a baseball cap when she cooks, always sponsored her son's baseball team. When the battle for civil rights was at its peak and it was illegal for blacks and whites to share public facilities, mixed-race groups of activists could gather at her place because the police wouldn't want to cross Mrs. Chase. And there was always a table for musicians and African American artists like Jacob Lawrence and Elizabeth Catlett, who would hang their work on her walls.

Traveling musicians knew a visit to New Orleans would not be complete without a stop at Dooky's. "We fed all of them," she said. "King Cole, Count Basie, Duke Ellington, everybody. Everybody came. Cab Calloway. Lena Horne. Sarah Vaughan. She was a sweetheart. Sarah came all the time."

Ray Charles, who was particularly fond of her red beans, liked the place so much that he slipped in a mention when he recorded Louis Jordan's "Early in the Mornin'":

I went to Dooky Chase to get me something to eat.
The waitress looked at me and said,
"Ray, you sure look beat." Now it's early in the morning
and I ain't got nothing but the blues.

Of course, time changed things. A new generation of eaters went looking for food more sophisticated than the homey Creole dishes Mrs. Chase cooked. She remodeled in the 1980s, but business still continued to drop. The neighborhood turned dangerous, although Mrs. Chase will probably not like that I used that word. But she would understand my point. The restaurant is in a neighborhood of small houses and just across the street from the Lafitte housing project. After Hurricane Katrina, it was shut down. The government fitted steel plates over doors and windows. Before the storm, she pulled a lot of customers from the 896 units there. But anyone could see the effects of drugs and unemployment and poverty on the neighborhood. People were always asking her why she didn't move, but she found dignity among people who had to make do with not much money. And when things were really bad, in the 1980s and early '90s, Mrs. Chase felt like she and her restaurant helped keep the neighborhood going.

"If we would have moved off this corner," she said, "this whole community would have been gone a long time ago."

But she hadn't counted on Hurricane Katrina, the storm that drowned her restaurant and most of her city.

The first time I ever spoke to Mrs. Chase was on a cell phone. It was a couple of weeks after the storm. She had evacuated to Baton Rouge. At that time, no one knew how long it would take to get the city back on its feet.

"What do you plan to do?" I asked.

"Oh, I'll be back," she said. "I have to come back. Who else is going to cook for them? If I don't get back in the kitchen, what message am I sending?"

By "them" she meant the people in her neighborhood. But she also meant everyone in New Orleans. No one knew it would be two years before she could get her restaurant cleaned up enough to start serving meals again, and even then she would only be running on fumes. People donated hundreds of thousands of dollars and kitchen equipment. Friends and fans of her food showed up to help. There were headaches with contractors and materials. And when she finally got things inside cleaned up, finding people who would work the restaurant the way she wanted it proved difficult. It still is, even though every day business gets a little better.

The first time I stood in front of Dooky Chase, it was still slimy with flood water and looked for all the world like another bowl of gumbo would never come from its kitchen.

A day earlier, I'd found one of the last seats on a plane full of volunteers and evacuated flood victims heading from New York to Louisiana. It had been three weeks since Katrina, and no one except rescue workers, soldiers and a handful of reporters were allowed inside the city limits. My friend Pableaux Johnson, who calls himself "your Cajun grandma with a beard," told me he would borrow a truck and help me work my way into the city. He was born and raised in Louisiana. He's also a good, enthusiastic cook and a food writer who is always up for an adventure. But mostly, Pableaux is a lover of his people. And his people, especially right after the storm, expanded almost daily to include those of us who fell into his orbit.

When Katrina hit, he had been living in a rambling apartment in Uptown, one of the few slivers of New Orleans proper that stayed dry. He evacuated to St. Martinville, a little town that sits nearly in the center of Louisiana Cajun country on Bayou Teche. Pableaux owns a small wooden church there. He converted it into a house and put in a big kitchen where the altar used to be. A couple of months before the hurricanes of 2005, Pableaux published *Eating New Orleans,* an intensely detailed guide on how to work your way through the city's tables.

"Basically, I wrote the guidebook for eating in Atlantis," he told me as we climbed into his truck.

The city had been closed since the levees failed, and Pableaux had been scrambling to take care of his own big, extended family and all the hurricane refugees who ended up at his church. But he was aching to check on his New Orleans apartment and his friends' places, so when I told him I was heading down to cover the culinary aftermath of Hurricane Katrina, he offered to be my Sacagawea. We headed out from the church just a little past three A.M., hoping to make the drive in a couple of hours and get to work before it got light.

We came up on New Orleans from the backside, slipping into a city that was closed along a road we could barely find in the dark. As we crept along, the headlights hit a young man with his hand up. We slowed to a stop. He stepped over broken tree branches and walked toward the pickup. For a split second, he looked like a teenager lost in the dark of a New Orleans night, except he was holding a rifle. When he got close enough, I made out his National Guard uniform. His unit was one of dozens that set up checkpoints around the city. His job was to keep people out until it was safe. I handed over my *Times* identification card and a letter from my newspaper that stated I was there on bona fide news-reporting business. He waved us on, and Pableaux drove into the dark city, navigating around abandoned buses and fallen trees and trying not to hit the stray, hungry dogs that roamed the street.

We spent the morning checking on his friends' homes and his own apartment. Every house we saw had fresh spray-painted circles bisected with Xs. In each quadrant, there was a number or a letter. One indicated the date the house was searched, another the organization that did the search, and yet another the number of bodies found inside. Animal rescuers had roamed the city with cans of paint, too. They were much less discreet, sometimes covering a good portion of the front of a house with entirely unhelpful messages like, "Cute brown dog found here. Was hungry." In the weeks after the city reopened, pet owners were left to puzzle out where their animals ended up with only those cryptic notes for clues.

The flooded, empty city had been baking for almost three weeks in 90-degree heat. Each time we got out of the truck, a stench would hit us so hard we pulled our T-shirts up over our noses. It was the airborne muck from maggoty food and leathery patches of mud and algae mixed with gasoline and an untraceable stink that was not unlike a rotting sneaker filled with Époisses. After a day or two saturated with that smell, you had to throw out your boots and clothes.

We got to Mrs. Chase's restaurant by mid-morning. The streets were so quiet it made us jumpy. About five feet up from the wall, a water line circled the building like a sad halo. It was deep green at the top and faded to brown closer to the sidewalk, marking the water level as the floodwater slowly receded from the neighborhood. The mix of seawater and wind had stripped the leaves from trees and sucked the green from the grass, so everything looked like a black-and-white movie. A rusting fryer basket was on its side just near the front door. Not too far away a paperback copy of the Dooky Chase cookbook, its pages swollen open and splattered with mud, lay on the sidewalk.

When the storm came, Mrs. Chase had a freezer full of gumbo and crab, the same way she had forty years earlier, when Hurricane Betsy killed eighty-one people and injured more than 17,000. Back then, with no electricity, she knew it would all go bad. But she still had gas, so she cooked up everything she had and worked with the police so she could deliver her food to people stranded in their homes. Hurricane Katrina was different. Water breached the levees and flooded her restaurant before she could blink an eye.

As we stood in front of Dooky Chase, the smell from the rotting food in her walk-in coolers mixed with the swampy, stenchy flood-water that still pooled here and there. Little flies hovered around the restaurant, swarming out of grass so gray and dry it crunched when you stepped on it. Someone had broken in and made off with the liquor and the cash register, but her precious collection of African American art had been spared, hung too high on the walls for the water to get to it and not immediately important to people looking for food, booze or cash.

"Damn," Pableaux kept saying. "Damn."

I bowed my head and said a little prayer.

Of all the potentially embarrassing things I've told you so far in this book, the fact that I pray every day is the one I used to be the most sheepish about. All that drinking until I passed out? No problem. Pull up a chair and let me tell you some war stories! But confessing that I believe in God? That's much harder for me to talk about.

I'm not a big Jesus freak or anything. My prayers are pretty simple. In the morning, I might say, "OK, God, here we go." And at night, especially after a bad day, I just say, "Oh well." I ask for some direction and the power to do the next right thing. I try to open my heart up a little more so the next day will be better. I don't tell many people I do this, especially the food people who make up the bulk of my professional life. Most of the food people I've known tend to get uncomfortable if you start talking about God and prayer unless you do it with irony or nostalgia. I know I used to. You might even be getting itchy right now.

Since I started making a living writing about people who grow and cook food, I've been invited to say grace—or even just pause for a minute to thank something bigger than us—maybe a dozen times before we all started eating. That's out of thousands of professional meals, and not counting Thanksgiving or Seder or dinner at my mother's house. But if you think about it, cooking and eating require the most consistent daily acts of faith of any activity, short of going to sleep and believing you'll wake up in the morning.

Each meal contains a thousand little divine mysteries. Who figured out that some beets should be golden, some red and others colored like candy canes? What blessed entity invented sugar and cacao pods and vanilla beans or figured out that salt can preserve and brighten anything? What are we to make of a hundred little lettuces and gnarled apples with so many names you can't remember them all? Who created melons and pork fat and peanuts, for crying out loud? And what of the miracle that is cheese?

Things get more mysteriously divine if you start to think about baking. Or how oil and garlic and egg yolk can make a glimmering, thick aioli. Mixing hot stock into a cold roux so it won't make lumps or mixing cake ingredients in the right order—butter and sugar together first, then eggs, then an alternating mix of flour and milk— are but two of the grand mysteries of the kitchen we blindly believe in. And we believe because someone told us the recipes would work. And so, on faith, we tried them. And once we tried them, and we saw that they worked, we became believers even though we had no idea how they worked. We spread the word to others who then tried them on faith, too. They became believers. Entire culinary cultures have been built on this kind of faith and trust.

Maybe you want to argue that all of the magic of the kitchen can be explained away in the cold scientific light of day. It isn't God but yeast that makes bread rise. A properly braised short rib is the result of a predictable release of collagen in heated connective tissue, not some deity that believes a sticky, glistening sauce can teach us about the beauty of the human condition.

Fine. So let's move to something you can't use science to argue about. Can the cold facts of the natural world explain that magic moment that comes when everyone at the table has just settled in to eat? Or the one that comes just when the delirious rush of sharing a good meal has ended? We sit around like grinning, milk-drunk babies who've just pulled away from the breast. Laughing comes easy. People glow. Out of nowhere, you have compassion for the jerk who was bugging you before dinner, so you ask if he'd like seconds on the braised artichokes. You belong to everyone else at the table and they belong to you.

You can't create that kind of communion alone, and you can't create it without food. That one moment ought to be proof to anyone that something greater than us is at work. It's a big part of why I have faith, but it doesn't explain why I pray my ass off every day. That's because it is the only way I have figured out not to have another drink. And trust me, no one wants me to have another drink.

Still, ever since that day in Alaska when I started praying, I have fought the complete embarrassment that comes when I talk about it outside of a circle of people who feel the same way I do. I felt like it made me weak, somehow. The big intellectuals I knew would surely scoff. Opiate of the masses and all that. It didn't help that I had grown up feeling the brunt of prejudice from people who use God to argue that I and my millions of gay and lesbian brothers and sisters should have no children, no civil rights and no happy eternity. In our household, Katia is the skeptical one. She knows that my believing in God keeps me sober, and she doesn't argue with that. And sometimes, she suspects there's even more to it. Like maybe there is a higher power. "Well, I hope you're right," she'll say.

But why was I so gun-shy about talking about it openly? Why couldn't I be more like Mrs. Chase, who will tell you without a blink that God is behind her every move. In the year after Katrina, I would check in on her by phone, keeping track of how she was getting along. In every conversation, she told me straight up front and center that she prayed every day, and that she had a lot of work to do. But it would get done, she said. God would see to it.

Mrs. Chase believes in a God who has all the answers, and really wants what's best for her. This is a bold statement coming from a woman who grew up in a segregated country that would not allow her to vote or mix too much with white people. She is a woman who watched her city and Dooky Chase, the restaurant where she had been cooking for more than sixty years, drown mostly due to a greedy and corrupt government. But still she has faith. And she has the kind of faith I longed for: one that had been tested. In the ten years since my last drink, I had faced a lot of internal demons and few external ones. Maybe that was test enough. Maybe I just had to stop doubting my own experience regarding faith.

One sticky morning nearly a year after Katrina, I went looking for Mrs. Chase. I wanted to see how the restaurant was coming along, if she thought she might reopen soon. But I was also hoping to learn more about God. I found her in her FEMA trailer, which had been set up on a side street across from Dooky Chase. The trailer was so small that her husband had to stand outside when she cooked. Mrs. Chase had an infected sore on her leg, and she had to ease herself slowly along a path made out of plywood to get from the trailer to the curb. It would have made sense for her to retire, to move into one of the refurbished houses her children owned in the neighborhood. The mold, the gouging by the contractors, the impossibility of getting her infected leg properly treated in a city where the health care system had all but collapsed—any one of those things would have made lesser women walk away.

I wanted to understand why she stuck it out, and how her faith got her through the devastation of Katrina. I wanted to see if through her story, I could find the strength to believe in my own. I asked her how she found the stamina to get back up when it all seemed so impossible. How did she not just crumble?

"The strong have feelings just like the weak, but they just don't show it," she said. Besides, she said, Katrina wasn't the worst thing that ever happened to her. She had lost a child.

Her beloved eldest daughter, Emily, her right hand and the woman most likely to carry on all the traditions and knowledge Mrs. Chase had accumulated, died giving birth to her eighth child in 1990. That child died a short time later after complications from the birth. The day after her daughter died, Mrs. Chase was scheduled to open the restaurant at eleven A.M. So she did. "I lost myself in the pots," she wrote in her memoirs. That day, I asked her why. "I could not put my sorrow on the whole world," she told me. "Life goes on, and that's what we have to understand with Katrina."

I pushed her for a better explanation. You don't come across eighty years' worth of courage very often. I needed to understand where her strength—her faith—came from. She didn't mind elaborating, using a baseball analogy.

"I tell people all the time, I think God is just like a pitcher," she said. And He apparently favors the low, slow curveball.

"It's a fun thing to see. It's a hard thing to hit," she explained. "But if you work on hitting this low, slow curve, it's going over the fence. It's going out of here. So I just think that God pitches us a low, slow curve. But He doesn't want us to strike out. I think everything he throws at you is testing your strength."

But Katrina?

"I tell you, I think I had more tears in the gumbo pot than I had gumbo," she said. "But you just cry and you just keep moving. It's not fair to put your hurt on somebody else." And then she said something remarkable. Maybe God flooded New Orleans to show man his mistakes.

"When you saw those people floating around in water, you saw every mistake you made. You had too many people in this city who couldn't fend for themselves. Where were we? Why were we not directing these people?" she said. "The levees broke on us, but we had many warnings, many times before. Why were we not checking those levees out after each warning?"

Like anyone who was there, the images from those first few days still fill her head. She says she has heard people—her own neighbors, even—say God brought his wrath down on poor black people because they weren't living right. Or, they said, God just doesn't like people of color. After all, the rich white folks in the Garden District didn't get flooded out and didn't lose their family members and their homes. But Mrs. Chase sees it differently.

"Look at it this way," she told me as we sat in a back room at Dooky Chase. "If we would have been saved on this end, and the French Quarter and all the big, beautiful homes Uptown would have been destroyed, look what a predicament we would be in. We couldn't help them up."

Maybe the rich people were saved, she said, because they had the resources to help the poor people get back on their feet. If all the rich people had been washed away, no one would have been left to help the poor.

"Don't you see how good things work? No matter how bad it is, good things work."

Even now, when I'm on the floor, feeling scraped down to bare metal, I think about what she told me. And I try to follow her pre- scription: "Figure out what you have to do in life and then just go to work and do it. Look at your world as a beautiful world. And it is a beautiful world. It's just your job to make it a little bit better."

I figure I can do that. I can make the world a little bit better. They say religion is for people who are afraid of hell and spirituality is for people who have been through it. Even though I haven't been through a hurricane or lost a daughter, I have had my own little trip to hell. And I know I will have more trials. When I do, like Leah Chase and millions of other people on this earth, I will pray. With- out shame and with an open heart.

On Holy Thursday, I made Mrs. Chase's gumbo z'herbes. It is a dish that requires faith. All recipes do, really. You have to trust the people who came before you, who burned a few things and threw out a few bowls of bad stuff in pursuit of a perfect dish. But in my interpretation of faith, whether recipe-based or soul-based, you have to have enough inner strength to change things up if you need to. God will send the directions, but you have to take the right steps.

The dish is served on Holy Thursday because for Catholics, that's the last day you get to eat a big meal before Easter. Catholics, my mother included, wouldn't eat meat on Good Friday. Those who hewed even closer to the faith would fast altogether. So you needed a good, meaty meal on Thursday to get you through to Saturday noon, when people would start eating normally again. Some food historians tie gumbo z'herbes to the African-Caribbean dish callaloo, but there is some indication it really has its roots in the Lutherans who settled in southern Louisiana in the 1800s and made a green vegetable soup for Holy Thursdays.

There is often a point when I'm cooking a new recipe that I panic. Sometimes it's just for a second, when a sauce isn't thickening or a batter seems suspiciously thin. I often start by blaming the person who wrote the recipe, assuming they didn't tell me that I need to whisk something for an extra few minutes or they left out an essential half cup of flour. Then, quickly, I turn the blame on myself for either hurrying through a step or doing something boneheaded like adding cayenne instead of paprika. I can be easily distracted, burning toast if the breakfast conversation is just too engaging. But I am also the kind of cook who can pull herself out of the culinary shame spiral pretty quickly, bravely plowing forward and hoping that some combination of good ingredients, strong kitchen fundamentals and a well-written recipe will allow me to pull off almost any dish.

Still, it was all I could do a few days before Easter to believe the thin, murky green swamp that filled my two biggest pots was going to taste any good at all.

My kitchen in Brooklyn is kind of a puffed-up galley, with a nice back door that opens to a patio. There is enough counter space to make my friends in their tiny Chelsea apartments jealous of the setup, although those same counters elicit pity from my friends in the suburbs out West. I had plowed through Mrs. Chase's recipe, and my small kitchen told the tale. It was as if a chlorophyll bomb had gone off. The sink was covered with trimmings from nine different greens, including carrot tops, collards and kale and a half head of lettuce I had in the fridge. Cutting boards held the remnants of ham, chopped brisket and andouille, smoked dark with pecan wood. In the two big pots, water seasoned with raw garlic and onions boiled. I had made a soft, brown roux in the grease from the hot sausage, and I had simmered a ham hock to make stock. I had pureed and pureed and pureed until everything was covered in green splatters, and the pots that once held ham stock now were filled with what smelled like a swamp with hints of forest fire.

Sara Roahen, an excellent cook and writer I met in New Orleans, spent some time cooking gumbo with Mrs. Chase. She recounts the experience in her fine, sweet book *Gumbo Tales: Finding My Place at the New Orleans Table*, which she wrote before and after Katrina. I called her when I was panicked over Mrs. Chase's gumbo recipe. There are several versions floating around, in Mrs. Chase's books and others. Sara's version begins with the warning that your kitchen will be a disaster. And she was right.

There I was, with two huge pots filled with muck. The thyme and salt and cayenne tasted raw and out of balance. It was too hot, maybe, or too bitter. I hadn't used Our Holy Mother of Lowry's Seasoning Salt, one of the great saints of the New Orleans spice rack. Maybe I used the wrong greens or should have added the chicken, like Sara advised.

"I think you just have to go with it," Sara said.

She was right. I said a little prayer and called people to the table. I had faith. Turns out the gumbo was awesome. It just needed time to come together.

———

This recipe is my slightly tweaked version of Sara's recipe, which is a tweaked version of Mrs. Chase's. I have tasted both Mrs. Chase's and Sara's. They are both delicious, but different. Yours will be, too. This is cooking, not an assembly line. Just have a little faith in your own skill and in the experience of the cooks who went before you. Sara says that in every cookbook where the gumbo appears, the recipe requires an odd number of greens, say five or seven or nine, for luck. Don't get too worried about that. Mrs. Chase told Sara that the connection between the kinds of greens and luck isn't really that big a deal. Just select at least seven of the greens listed, although you can use what you have. But make sure the pile of greens seems like way too much to start.

GUMBO Z'HERBES

1 large or 2 small ham shanks or hocks
At least 7 varieties of the following greens:

1 bunch greens, either mustard, collard or turnip or a combination of
    all three

1 bag fresh spinach or a box of frozen

1 small head cabbage

1 bunch carrot tops

1 bunch beet tops

1 bunch arugula

1 bunch parsley

1 bunch green onions

1 bunch watercress

1 head romaine or other lettuce

1 head curly endive

1 bunch kale

1 bunch radish tops

3 medium yellow onions, roughly chopped

½ head garlic, peeled, cloves kept whole

2 pounds fresh hot sausage (a local sausage called chaurice is best, but hot
    Italian without fennel works well)

1 pound andouille sausage

1 pound smoked pork sausage

½ pound ham

1 pound beef stew meat

1 cup flour

Vegetable oil as needed

3 teaspoons dried thyme

2 teaspoons cayenne pepper

3 bay leaves

Salt to taste

2 cups cooked white rice

½ teaspoon filé powder (optional)

1. Place ham shanks or hocks in a large, heavy stockpot. Fill the pot with water and bring to a boil; reduce heat and simmer while you prepare the other ingredients.
2. Wash all greens thoroughly in salt water, making sure to remove any grit, discolored outer leaves, and tough stems. Rinse in a bath of unsalted water (a clean double sink works well for this).
3. Place half the greens, half the onions, and half the garlic in a heavy-bottomed stockpot or 3 to 4 gallon saucepan. Cover greens and vegetables with water and bring to a boil over high heat; reduce heat to a simmer and cook for 20 to 30 minutes, until greens are very tender. When they finish cooking, transfer them to a large bowl, using a slotted spoon, to cool. Repeat the process with the remaining greens, onions and garlic, doing it in two or three batches if necessary.
4. When all the greens have finished cooking, reserve the cooking liquid.
5. Place the fresh hot sausage in a skillet or medium-size saucepan and set over medium heat. Cook until rendered of fat and moisture. Remove the hot sausage with a slotted spoon and set aside. Reserve the fat.
6. While the hot sausage is cooking, cut the andouille and smoked sausage into ½-inch rounds and set aside. Cut the ham and the beef stew meat into ½-inch pieces and set aside.
7. In a meat grinder or a food processor, grind the greens, onion and garlic into a puree, adding cooking liquid to prevent the greens from getting too thick. Do this in batches.
8. Remove the ham shanks from their cooking liquid,

reserving the liquid for stock. Once the shanks cool, pick and chop the meat and set it aside; discard the bones and the fat.

9. Pour the greens cooking liquid and ham stock into separate bowls. Using your largest pot, or the two stockpots in which you simmered the greens and the ham, mix everything together. (Divide the pureed greens, the sausages, the beef and the chopped ham equally between the two pots, if using two pots.)

10. Fill the pot or pots with equal parts ham stock and greens cooking liquid and bring to a simmer over medium-high heat.

11. Heat the skillet containing the hot sausage drippings over medium-high heat. With a wooden spoon, slowly but intently stir in the flour until well combined. If the mixture is very dry, add vegetable oil until it loosens some, making a tight paste that's still able to be stirred.

12. Continue to cook until the flour mixture begins to darken, stirring constantly. As Sara notes, you aren't going for a dark roux, but you do want the flour to cook. Courage is the key here. Don't be afraid to let it get dark.

13. When darkened and cooked, divide the roux between the two stockpots or put it into the single pot, dropping it in by spoonfuls and whisking to make sure that each is well incorporated.

14. Add thyme, cayenne, bay leaves and salt to taste.

15. Simmer for about an hour, or until the stew meat is tender, stirring quite often. Add more stock or water if it appears too thick.

16. Serve over white rice.

162 * KIM SEVERSON

NOTE: Filé in its pure form is a bright green powder made from pounded sassafras leaves. The Creoles and Cajuns picked it up from the Choctaw Indians, and used it as a spice and a thickener in the winter when okra wasn't available. If you like it, add it slowly at the end of cooking or even stir it into your own bowl at the table. Sara reports that Mrs. Chase told her, "It'll lump up on you" if you're not careful. Mrs. Chase's father used to grind sassafras leaves for her, and she told Sara that Creoles always add filé to their gumbo z'herbes, even if few cookbook recipes call for it.

Yield: *Enough for a dozen or so people to have dinner, and maybe a little left over for the freezer.*

7

Blood and Water

When you wake up, you never know if the day might end up meaning everything. It could be the day you meet your wife or the day you put down your last drink or the day your baby is born. Sometimes, what happens is so subtle that you don't even realize how important the day was until years later. That's how it was on a hot early summer afternoon in Georgia, when I held the hand of Miss Edna Lewis.

We were in the small kitchen in an apartment she shared with a young chef named Scott Peacock. Like me, Scott is gay. Miss Lewis was already wrapped in the physical pain of old age and the mental fog that comes with it. She didn't speak a word to me directly that day, and she died nine months after I met her. But looking back, I can see that our meeting marked an important milestone in a journey that would end when I finally understood something that had been my greatest source of strength and my greatest source of pain: my glorious and imperfect family.

I suspected early on that I was gay. There were the deep crushes at summer camp and the teacher I really, really liked. At first, those feelings could easily be brushed off. But by high school, I knew for sure. How? Well, the same way most people know they are heterosexual. You get crushes. You play the same song over and over, thinking only of the object of your obsession. It all works the same.

Perhaps you're wondering if I ever, uh, experienced what I might be missing. I did have some awkward attempts at heterosexuality when I was younger. I still feel bad for Ricky, the unwitting foreign exchange student who took me to the prom thinking he might get lucky. There were other forays onto that side of the playing field, some of them unwanted and most of them fortified with a few pitchers of beer.

Of course, it took a little time to digest what as a teenager seemed like a terrifying piece of knowledge. Everything around me suggested that the strange, excited feeling I had every time I saw Marcia on *The Brady Bunch* was best not described to anyone. No one at home or at school ever presented it as an option. And although I can't recall ever hearing a gay slur at home, I endured enough taunts at school to realize being a lesbian might not be such a great thing to tell people. Don't misunderstand. Unlike some gay kids, I didn't think, That's sick. I've got to change. I knew I wasn't going to change. I didn't want to change. But I knew instinctively that it'd be better all the way around if I just didn't say anything. A piece of information like that would bring on a world of hurt. My parents would be so disappointed. And I couldn't have that. So a life of secrets began in earnest.

The problem was that keeping such a big part of my life from my family was a lot of work. And ultimately, it was heartbreaking. I had to find the strength and the understanding to bring the two parts of my life together.

I knew I would meet Miss Lewis from the moment I saw her framed photograph on the long hallway wall in Marion Cunningham's California ranch house. In it, she is sitting in the sun with Marion, looking the same as she does on the covers of her cookbooks and in nearly every other photograph I have seen of her since—her bun always loose at the nape of her neck, her head just barely tilted back, her face painted with an enigmatic smile that makes Mona Lisa look like Jim Carrey. It's an odd thing, but somehow, on a purely intuitive level, I knew she had answers—that she knew about family and cooking and life and that, somehow, our very different worlds would come together.

In many ways, Miss Lewis was the last direct link to a way of cooking and eating that began in the soft Virginia soil where she grew up. Just a generation beyond slavery, she was one of six children. She was born in a small settlement called Freetown in 1916 and had a life that was deeply rooted in a sense of place. Miss Lewis learned to cook at a time when what came out of the ground was what you had to work with. As a result, she was always a resourceful cook, believing in the purity of the ingredients and taking a lead from nature on what to eat and when to eat it. Growing, gathering and preparing food was more than just sustenance for the family; it was a form of entertainment. Without fancy cooking equipment, the family improvised, measuring baking powder on coins and cooking everything over wood.

The life she would later write about in her books centered on cooking for Baptist revivals, holidays or just because it was morning and a family breakfast on a farm in the South matters. Almost every meal was to be shared. In that way, we had something else in common. It didn't take me long to figure out that the best way to find a place in my family was to be as close to the kitchen as possible.

"Whenever I go back to visit my sisters and brothers, we relive old times, remembering the past," Miss Lewis wrote in the introduction to her second book, *The Taste of Country Cooking*. "And we share again in gathering wild strawberries, canning, rendering lard, finding walnuts, picking persimmons, making fruitcake, I realize how much the bond that held us together had to do with food."

Even though my brothers and my sister all live in different cities, we share a tight bond. And the language of that bond is often the language of food. Some of them still fight it, refusing to cook a big holiday meal or picking fast food over their own kitchen, but we are a family that will end up together at the table. And that's what attracted me to Miss Lewis. James Beard said her food represented a time when American cooking was a series of family events. To me, that's the best kind of cooking to do. You can cook when you're hungry or cook to make a living or to feel creative or even just as a distraction, but cooking for the people whom you wake up with and go to sleep with is the best thing ever.

Miss Lewis's recipes, for dishes like minted peas and creamed ham and cucumber pickles and hickory nut cookies, came from a time when ice had only a cameo role and was used mostly to churn ice cream. If something couldn't be eaten right away, it went into the springhouse over the stream or it was preserved and canned for later. Recipes were developed to accommodate tender lettuces that had to be picked young before they "bolted," or became bitter when they went to seed prematurely in the hot sun. That lettuce was best, she believed, served with gently assertive young scallions and a special dressing with vinegar and sugar and a little salt and pepper. Oil would weigh down the tender leaves.

"I feel fortunate to have been raised at a time when the vegetables from the garden, the fruit from the orchard, and the meat from the smokehouse were all good and pure, unadulterated by chemicals and long-life packaging," she wrote in *The Taste of Country Cooking*. "As a result, I believe I know how food should taste. So now, whether I am experimenting with a new dish or trying to recapture the taste of a simple, old-fashioned dish, I have that memory of good flavor to go by."

In that book and in her third, *In Pursuit of Flavor*, you can learn about a kind of Southern cooking that erases all of your ideas about it. I guess I thought I knew about Southern food, but it was a cartoon version. I had eaten plenty of chicken-fried steaks and beans and barbecue in the cowboy corners of Houston when I was a kid. During the few years I spent living around Oakland, I always circled back to a handful of urban soul food spots and rib joints. But that is not what Miss Lewis would consider Southern food. She hated the term *soul food*. Inner-city restaurants that served watery greens and greasy fried chicken and dull macaroni and cheese were a bastardization of real, true Southern cooking and, to her mind, didn't represent anything good. I didn't know how much I didn't know about Southern cooking until I started reading what Miss Lewis had written. Soon it spoke to me in a way that is second only to the food of Italy.

People have come to call Miss Lewis the grande dame of Southern cooking, but the biggest piece of her cooking career was in New York. She had been drawn to the city because of its politics and culture. Politics were very important to Miss Lewis. She had been the first in her family to vote, and said her greatest honor was to work for Franklin D. Roosevelt's first presidential race. Later, she would march with Dr. Martin Luther King at the Poor People's March in Washington in 1968. Her last cooking job was at a Brooklyn restaurant called Gage and Tollner, when she was in her seventies and by all rights should have been retired. But the most glamorous restaurant job came in the late 1940s and early 1950s, when she cooked at Café Nicholson on the ground floor of a brownstone on 52nd Street near Second Avenue on Manhattan's East Side. Wendell Brock, the longtime writer for the *Atlanta Journal-Constitution*, talked to her once about café society as she came to see it from her vantage point in the kitchen.

"We had everybody that was anybody," Miss Lewis told him. Howard Hughes, Salvador Dalí, Marlene Dietrich, Eleanor Roosevelt, Lillian Hellman and Dashiell Hammett all visited. When William Faulkner came in, the food impressed him so much that he asked Miss Lewis if she had studied in Paris. She was flattered. She had never been out of the United States.

Tennessee Williams lived nearby, so he sometimes walked her home at night. And Greta Garbo dropped in with her two little poodles. "She came on a Monday night when we were closed," Miss Lewis told Mr. Brock. "They dined by themselves. But by the time they got ready to go, the sidewalk was lined because the word had spread that it was Garbo."

Truman Capote was a regular. "He was a big mess," Miss Lewis recalled. "He had on these little pumps. If he got something new, he would come in and say, 'How do you like my beloved pants?' He was cute."

Although she was a great cook, she also had the ability to explain, in the simplest language, the beauty of food. A couple of years ago, Ruth Reichl had the good fortune of coming upon an essay

Miss Lewis had written on lined sheets of yellow paper in the 1990s, and published it in *Gourmet* magazine. The essay was Miss Lewis's attempt to describe what it means to be Southern. She wrote of the way her bare feet felt when they pushed against warm, just-plowed earth and the way a shroud of mist hangs low on a Southern spring morning. And she offered up a long and glorious list of dishes:

"Southern is a pitcher of lemonade, filled with sliced lemon and a big piece of ice from the ice house, and served with buttermilk cookies."

"Southern is a great yeast roll, the dough put down overnight to rise and the next morning shaped into rolls and baked. Served hot from the oven, they are light as a dandelion in a high wind."

"Southern is leftover pieces of boiled ham trimmed and added to a saucepan of heavy cream set on the back of the stove to mull and bring out the ham flavor, then served spooned over hot biscuits."

"Southern is a pot of boiling coffee sending its aroma out to greet you on your way in from the barn."

And, tucked among the lovely descriptions of food and her strikingly clear childhood memories, she writes this about the man with whom she would make the most unlikely family: "Southern is Scott Peacock, one of the South's most creative young chefs."

At first, Scott didn't want me at that kitchen table where Miss Lewis spent her last days drinking coffee and watching TV. He wasn't about to let some reporter just parade by her like she was an exotic bird at the zoo.

I had headed to Atlanta originally to write about fried chicken. Although Scott puts out impeccable versions of sharp pimento cheese, summer squash, biscuits and catfish, it was his fried chicken that was packing his restaurant, Watershed, in nearby Decatur. He owns it with Emily Saliers, one half of the Indigo Girls. The mixture of music and chicken was a hard one for me to pass by.

The chicken that comes out of the cast-iron pans in that kitchen is the perfect marriage of the cultures that Miss Lewis and Scott were born into. The recipe starts with a long soak in brine and then in buttermilk, which is how they do it in the part of southern Alabama where Scott was born and raised. Next comes a toss in seasoned flour. Then the pieces get slipped into a pan filled with lard and butter seasoned with a piece of Virginia ham, which is how Miss Lewis liked it.

I had eaten a big plateful of that chicken several months earlier when I was in Atlanta visiting friends. It was so good I had to find a way to get back to write about it. After a little digging around, I figured out that the story might be bigger than just fried chicken. It was about family, really. One that a gay white man from Alabama had created with a straight African American woman forty years his senior, with a famous lesbian folk singer thrown in for good measure.

So I traveled back to Atlanta to report the story. Scott was waiting for me in a coffee shop near his restaurant. He had plenty of reasons to be wary. For one thing, I would be asking a lot of questions, and publicity had not always turned out so well for him. And he knew I wanted to meet Miss Lewis. It was important for the story, sure. But I had personal reasons. She was among the great American women whom I admired because they cooked their way through life's ups and downs.

By the time I made it to Miss Lewis, she was almost ninety and very frail. She had dementia and spent most of her time in the apartment she shared with Scott. They didn't start out as a family. Miss Lewis was seventy-three when they met and still cooking in New

York. He was twenty-six and working as a chef at the Georgia governor's mansion. Scott was one of those young, tender men who thought all of the answers could be found in a bigger city, a bigger place—anywhere else but his small town. He had seen her picture in a magazine once, struck by how lovely she was. He'd even met her a few times, but he was sure she would never remember him. Then he was asked to help Miss Lewis cook at a fund-raising dinner in Atlanta. He was to meet her at the station when she got off the train from New York.

He spotted her at the end of the platform, walking toward him dragging a cardboard box wrapped in blue nylon rope. It was filled with one hundred pounds of pie dough. "I will never forget that," he said. "Here is that regal lady dragging this big ol' box of pie dough down the road."

Miss Lewis, who always tried to perfect whatever task she had at hand, figured there would not be enough time to make good pie dough. So she brought her own. Scott was swooning. Shortly after that, he gave up trying to cook seasonal food inspired by France or Italy—it was the fashion at the time—and decided he should cook Southern. It meant getting over his notion that Southern food was poor food and that cooking it meant embracing his childhood.

"It really was a Paul-on-the-road-to-Damascus moment," he said.

Miss Lewis had shown him he did not have to run from his past, but that there was strength in embracing it. And that set them off on a lifelong relationship, one that would eventually help me understand how my past—my family—was actually my greatest strength.

Miss Lewis eventually moved to Atlanta, where they worked together to preserve Southern food. They wrote a book. Then she developed some medical problems. Scott took care of her. And it started to dawn on him how much she meant to him.

"Aside from someone I was seeing at the time, she was the person I thought about the most and related to the most," he said. "I do remember at some point being very clear that she understood me in a way that other people didn't and later feeling that I felt that way about her, too."

He began to realize they had the makings of something that looked an awful lot like a family. She was his first phone call in the morning, and they would speak throughout the day. "We became increasingly dependent on each other," he said. Miss Lewis had come to rely on Scott to record and keep alive her knowledge of Southern cooking, but she was also coming to rely on him for her health and well-being. Scott would worry if she was taking her medicine or if her refrigerator was full. And Miss Lewis liked doing small, loving things for him, like ironing his shirts or making him little gifts. It was unconditional, which is really what we all want from our families, right?

She saw him for who he could be, and she helped him accept who he was. "I was a success as a chef before Miss Lewis," he said, "but I was a failure as a human being."

His love for Miss Lewis was the power he needed to get over his fears and anxieties. And it was that love that carried him through the slow progression of days to her death, which was in the very apartment the two first moved into and in which Scott still lives.

So you can see why Scott was so wary the day I asked to meet her. "I was worried what you would think if she was having one of those days when she was asleep at the table," he told me later. "I didn't want you to see her if she was having a bad day. I hate that—when it's like walking people through there to see the panda, the icon in a wheelchair. Laying eyes on her just to lay eyes on her seemed creepy."

Besides, surprise visitors can upset a person with dementia. "People think if they can just make them remember the one right thing it will all come flooding back," Scott said. "But it doesn't work that way. It just makes them more agitated."

Scott had other reasons to feel protective. Months earlier, members of her biological family had challenged Scott's place in her life. They took him to court. The whole mess started after Alice Waters approached Scott at a wedding they had both been invited to. Alice had been good friends with Miss Lewis. Like so many women in that elite circle of cooks, Alice worried about what would happen to the generation of cooks just ahead of her when they got old. Here they were, Marion Cunningham and Edna Lewis and Julia Child and a dozen other women who were the stars of their culinary generation, and they were all frail and dying. Who would take care of them?

A few chefs with big restaurants or television shows or the special fortunes of Julia Child might be rich, but that's the exception. Great cooks who mostly cook and write great books, especially the ones of Miss Lewis's generation, end up much poorer than people imagine and can't provide for themselves once they can't cook or write anymore.

Miss Lewis's money came mostly from her books. In the late 1960s, she was sidelined with a broken leg after a fall on an icy New York street. To pass the time, she began writing out some recipes and it turned into her first book, *The Edna Lewis Cookbook*. Her next, *The Taste of Country Cooking*, would become a classic study of Southern cooking, and one that sits on the shelves of America's best chefs. It helped put an end to the knee-slapping, cornpone image of Southern food among many American cooks. Her last book was with Scott, called *The Gift of Southern Cooking*. It would become her best-selling work. But even lumped together, the books never made

enough money to provide for her care as she aged. Scott could barely
shoulder the financial burden of taking care of her alone.

Alice knew this, and she told Scott that people who admired Miss
Lewis wanted to help. So he agreed to set up a fund through the
Georgia Community Trust to pay for some of her care. Another sup-
porter drafted a letter appealing for help, a copy of which made its way
to her relatives in Virginia. That was a turning point in what had been
a distant but respectful relationship between Scott and her family.

Her younger sister, Ruth Lewis Smith, and some other family
members, including a son from Africa she had adopted when he
was an adult, asked a probate judge in Decatur to decide whether
Miss Lewis should live in Unionville, Virginia, with her siblings, or
stay with Scott. "I told him I am willing to take care of her, you need
not ask for money," Mrs. Smith told me. "I think he would respect
Edna by letting her come home."

She and other family members and a few friends made it clear
that they were very uncomfortable having someone who was not a
blood relation caring for an ailing relative. That he was a young man
responsible for an elderly woman made them uncomfortable. Perhaps that he was white made them uncomfortable. Perhaps it was
that he was a ho-mo-SEX-u-al, as some said when I called.

But Scott knew she wanted to stay with him. Miss Lewis had told
him so. Now that I have known Scott for some years, I know that he
would have taken her back to Virginia in a New York minute if she
had asked him to. But that day we met, I had no idea whether to
believe him and his story about the court case, about her health and
about the family he said they had created, just him and Miss Lewis.

"So would it be possible to meet her?" I asked. "Just to say
hello?"

"I'm sorry," he said. "Miss Lewis just isn't that well today."

After a couple hours of talk both about work and about our-selves, we said our good-byes outside the coffee shop. There was no need to play hardball. This wasn't a corrupt government official or someone asking for money. They were just a couple of cooks. My story would be fine without laying eyes on her. I got into the rental car and started the engine. Then Scott was at the window. He had had a change of heart.

"Would you like to meet her?" he asked.

I followed him into their apartment. Miss Lewis sat at the table in their crowded kitchen. A little television sat on a corner of the table, tucked next to a sugar bowl and a glass filled with tiny violets. An episode of *The Little Rascals* flickered on the screen.

"Miss Lewis, this is Kim Severson from *The New York Times*," Scott said.

"Hello, Miss Lewis," I said and reached out.

She raised her hand to mine, and I held it. She looked at me with that enigmatic smile. I murmured something about what an honor it was to meet her. She nodded.

"Can I take your photograph with Miss Severson, Miss Lewis?" Scott asked.

She gave him a look and raised her eyebrows. I could barely hear her when she said no. Then she turned back to her show.

Scott explained later that the fade was slow at first, but that things got more difficult almost daily. As she slipped away, his de-spair worsened. Not much could pull her from that private fog in her last days. Nature sometimes would, but the little bit of moss or wildflowers Scott would bring in from the outdoors had become unreliable mood lifters. Even food, her beloved touchstone, wasn't doing much to stir her anymore.

As she grew increasingly feeble, Scott took precise care of her.

He would tease her when the dementia propelled her out of bed at night. He'd tuck her back in and say, "I don't want to come in here and find any strange men." If that didn't get a laugh, nothing would. But days would pass without even a glimmer of her old self.

One day, in a stroke of pure luck, he discovered something that could reach her. It had an almost medicinal effect on her mood and attentiveness. It was *The Little Rascals*, a series from the 1930s and '40s that featured little children running around and getting into trouble, including the controversial African American character called Buckwheat.

His first clue came when, watching television together, he noticed that Miss Lewis would perk up when children were on the screen. He tried different child-centric movies with no luck. Then he brought home *The Little Rascals* and Miss Lewis immediately brightened. She was her old self, even if just for the span of a television show.

"It was one of the happiest days," he said. They'd watch an episode together and laugh so hard they'd nearly hit the floor in tears. Sometimes at night, after he had helped her bathe, they'd walk down the hall, his arm entwined in hers.

"Let's see what the boys are doing," Scott would tell her.

Later he told me he thanked God for *The Little Rascals*.

During the trial, when her biological family was challenging Scott's care, that show became an issue. Her relatives' lawyer argued that exposing an old black woman to repeated episodes of a show that employed broad stereotypical images of African Americans was cruel and insensitive. It lacked dignity. And it proved Scott wasn't the right person to care for her. The judge didn't agree with that argument or others they made.

Miss Lewis would be allowed to die with Scott, which was, as best as outsiders could tell, what she wanted.

He knew the end was coming when her interest in food faded. One day, she poured curdled milk into her coffee and didn't know it. So Scott started making her beloved coffee for her. It was like communion for him. He would always heat the milk just so, and make sure it was all piping hot, just as she liked it. Then came the morning she had no interest in coffee at all. "That was so heartbreaking for me and so sad because all of that had been part of how we had communicated," he said.

In her last days, when she was in bed and so close to death he could feel it, he played her favorite music and coated her lips with honey and a bit of Virginia country ham so she could leave this earth with the flavors of her youth. Miss Lewis died on February 13, 2006. She was two months shy of her ninetieth birthday.

"I never fell out of awe with Edna Lewis," he told me later. "Even at the end when I was cleaning her and dressing her every day, even when she was a corpse at the funeral home, I would just look at her and connect. I would think, God, you are an incredible woman. How lucky am I? She was my family, most certainly."

It was kind of inevitable that Scott and I would later end up friends. For one thing, we share some major themes. We both don't drink. We love food. And we both knew we were big ol' homosexuals early on. He wanted an Easy Bake oven. I wanted a catcher's mitt. There's an informal social glue that sometimes forms among gays and lesbians because you are connected at a root level. You were both born different, and that makes you the same. In a world that expects and often demands heterosexuality, you both know the pain that can come when you just can't deliver. You share the scars from getting called a faggot or a dyke. You know what it's like to feel "other," even in your own family. Especially in your own family.

When you grow up in a family like his, where the threat of being exposed as a homosexual is used as a weapon, or like mine, where matters of sex, let alone homosexuality, aren't really discussed with anything approaching clarity, you quickly develop a secret life. And it can bring on a terrible feeling of never being good enough, of always being at risk of disappointing someone. It's something Scott and I share, and something we both have spent a lifetime trying to unlearn.

"If someone said they loved my shoes, I thought, Oh, they hate my pants," he told me during one of the long phone conversations that usually started with a recipe and ended with mutual psychoanalysis.

"If someone said something nice, of course, it was never enough," he said.

I'd counter with my own special version of the theme.

"Or how about this," I'd say. "No matter how good I am, it will never be enough to counter all the ways I just don't measure up. And if I don't measure up, I will never be seen." I always knew it was safe to talk about these things with Scott. Because, like me, he adores the family he was born into. We both know a lot of our pain comes from growing up gay in a house where there wasn't any room for it. But we also cherish the families that made us who we are.

In some large families, where there's one gay kid, there are often two. That was the case in mine. You can imagine my parents' surprise.

As a kid, even before we both knew we were gay, I was desperately close to my older brother Kent. We built forts out of plywood and ran through the woods together. But we fought like cowboys and Indians. Once, in a fit of anger that likely came after he wouldn't let me play with him and his friends, I beaned him with a big rotary dial phone. He's still got the scar over his lip. He would roll me in a blanket so I couldn't move and set me on the front lawn. But when I went away to summer camp, he was so brokenhearted he moped for days. And when he started his own short-lived experiments with the neighbor girls, I sat alone in our backyard fort, bereft and abandoned.

I had no real clue that he was gay when we were in high school. He was a top-ranked musician, a good-looking senior popular with the cheerleaders. I was an awkward freshman with a Texas accent trying to make the basketball team. How was I supposed to know? Later, after we were both out of the house, we came out to each other and formed a kind of gay subcommittee in the family. It's awesome to have a gay sibling. But it took time for us to get comfortable with each other. Years of training to just keep quiet and go about one's business in the sex department were hard to break.

In the end, my gay story is like that of most other people from my generation, which was post-Stonewall but pre-Ellen. I came of age just after the period when lesbians were fighting to be heard within the larger feminist movement of the 1970s and when AIDS was just starting to hit our gay brothers. Back then, there was no gay-straight alliance at my high school. They called me a lezzie in the halls a few times, but I don't think that counts. I knew not one openly gay person until I was a couple of years into college. So when I was in my most formative years, I simply had no context to make sense of what I was feeling. And I suspect my parents, both born in the 1930s to traditional religious families in small Midwestern towns, had none to offer on the matter, either.

I have to say right here that I really believe my parents did the best they could with the cards they were dealt. Sure, I wish it had been different. Who doesn't think that about their childhood? I see now that it wasn't easy for them. The gay thing, had they known, would have been the least of their worries during my teenage years. I was, simply put, a wild teenager. They shed a lot of tears over me, trying to keep me from sneaking out of the house and doing drugs. Who knows how it might have been if they knew what was really going on inside me, how alone and hurt I felt?

The overarching and stated theme for all the Severson children was that our parents just wanted us to be happy and grow up right. Whatever that meant. Besides, our big, active family demanded teamwork, not individualism. We were a suburban family, and appearances were to be kept. There would be no room for the flying of one's freak flag. We were to strive to move up in the world and to help make it a better place while we did it. Not bad values, in the long run. And at all costs, we were to put the family first. It was a very Italian thing, and one that would be the most enduring lesson of my childhood. You can see why I thought maybe I'd better just keep quiet about the whole liking girls thing.

Still, I couldn't wait to play house and begin to figure out what a family might look like if I could really be myself. My first inkling of that came in college with Cindy, my first girlfriend. We had met when we were both in high school, but later in college we would share a room in a house with ten other people, most of whom never did the dishes and always used my towel. It was the first of many times I would realize that maybe things at home weren't so bad after all.

To make rent and buy books, I made pizzas and fried eggs and waited tables and painted dorm rooms. But mostly we lived on politics and love and music. We got radical and took back the night and supported the rape crisis center and took womyn's study courses and generally united in uterine empathy against The Man. Cindy and I also met a lot of other women like us. This, of course, was when the trouble started. We had a dramatic and rocky breakup, but eventually got over it. Time is like that. Today we're best friends.

Toward the end of college, I finally got tired of hiding such a big part of myself from my parents. So, after a little free counseling from the college clinic, I wrote my mom The Letter. I imagine parents all over the country get The Letter eventually. I'm sure I'll get one, too. Someday, after Sammy has grown up and been to therapy and begins to figure herself out.

The Letter usually goes something like this:

> *Dear Mom and Dad,*
> *I am angry because* (fill in the offense here).
> *It makes me feel* (fill in the emotion here).
> *I am not sure when I can speak with you again.*
> *Signed,*
> *Your Child*

In the letter I wrote, I demanded that my mother acknowledge all sides of me. I refused to keep up the charade any longer. I was a lesbian and I would not stand for mere tolerance. No, I wanted complete acceptance. My poor mother.

I was, of course, terrified. The minute I sent it, I was sure it was a bad idea. I waited. We even had phone conversations, and neither of us mentioned it. I finally got a letter back on her embossed robin blue stationery.

"I know," she wrote. "I'm just not ready to talk about it." She signed it, "Love, Mommie."

For the next few years after college, we had a standoff of sorts. It was "don't ask, don't tell" at its best. I talked in vague code about my "roommates" and she stopped asking about boyfriends. As I started working and moved around the West Coast, our code evolved. Things softened between us. Once, my mother suggested I might like to meet a friend's daughter. "She's a bachelor lady, like you."

Time, of course, is a lovely balm. And to my parents' great credit, they treated each girlfriend whom I dragged home with great respect, even buying them little Christmas and birthday presents. Slowly, I stopped being so defensive and my parents started to accept that I wasn't going to change. But increasingly the fact that I had an entire life I couldn't talk about to my mother, let alone my father, was breaking my heart. I wasn't being truthful with them, and I didn't want to keep living a euphemistic life. Then, after yet another bad breakup, I ended up on my parents' couch, shattered. I didn't have the energy to keep up the euphemisms anymore. I poured out my heart to Mom, which is probably what she wanted all along. Just a little truth and a little trust. I mean, how could I blame her for not talking to me about this huge part of my life if I wasn't going to talk to her?

This even spilled over onto my father, a conservative man not given to emoting. "Well," my dad said to me during that trip home. "Your mother tells me you're having a hard time. I'm sorry it didn't work out."

It was Christmas dinner a few years ago when I realized just how far my family had come. My parents had always been open to all kinds of guests at the Christmas table, and over the years, it meant friends and lovers of their five children. That's fine by my mother, who likes to have a lot of people around the table. To her, Christmas is the Super Bowl of holidays. One would think the birth of the Baby Jesus would be enough, but as an added bonus she gets to cover the table in Spode Christmas dishes and antique candlestick holders, make both prime rib and fried baccalà with onions, and have as many of her children as she can fly in from thousands of miles away to wake up early and watch one another open presents, one grueling gift at a time.

Her refrain: "I just want us all to be together."

I have come to love Christmas in the Colorado mountains with my mother and father, even though the adjustment has not always been easy for my girlfriends. One particular Christmas, early in our relationship, I brought Katia, who is Jewish. That year, my brother brought his Turkish boyfriend. He happens to be Muslim.

This is so nice, I think. My parents have gotten over their initial surprise (a nice way of putting it) at having two gay children. I am in love. The crown rib roast is so rare it's like velvet, and the snow is falling gently. It's Christmas.

It was also a couple years after 9/11, and my father was a couple of martinis into his evening.

"So," he says, gesturing with his glass toward my brother's boyfriend, "why are your people flying planes into buildings?"

As I recall it, the snow suddenly stopped falling. A chill settled over the table. The candles might have even gone out. I can't be sure.

"Now, Jim," my mother says. "It's Christmas! Let's not talk about that."

"No, no. It's fine," my brother's boyfriend says. He launches into a long, historical lecture that begins with a deconstruction of Christianity and ends, essentially, with an argument that makes it all the Jews' fault.

At this point, I see the color slowly rising in my girlfriend's cheeks. She gets up to wash the dishes.

"Well," says my mother, "all of that happened a long time ago. Besides, it's Christmas!"

My brother and the boyfriend eventually broke up. Katia and I got married and now have a daughter. My brother is our baby's special protector. My father still doesn't understand the finer points of Middle East politics, and my mother still loves putting out the Spode china for Christmas.

And we all still are crazy for each other, bumping along through uncomfortable dinners and misunderstandings and all kinds of hurts. That's because we are family, both chosen and given. And that's why sometimes, like Scott did with Miss Lewis, you have to go start a new family before you can really love the one you came from.

A couple years after that Christmas and a few months after Miss Lewis died, Katia and I threw ourselves a big wedding in San Francisco. It wasn't a legal one, although we got married later when it was legal. (Then that marriage was put to a vote of the people, who decided that gays and lesbians shouldn't have a right to marry in California. So although it became illegal for gay people to marry in California, ours was deemed legal by the state supreme court. Please don't send another wedding gift.)

On that day, when our parents walked us down the aisle and we had the dances and the dinner and the cake, I felt different. I felt like I was finally a part of the family I had grown up with. All of me.

"Well," my mother said. "It's just like a real wedding."

And it was.

A year later, Katia and I had our little Sammy, conceived with the help of a sperm bank, carried by Katia and with both our names on the birth certificate. (Thank you, New York State adoption case law.) As much as Katia's love and my sobriety have changed my life, entire rooms in my heart opened up the day our daughter was born.

One afternoon when Sammy was just a few months old, I was on the telephone with Scott. I had the phone headset on and Sammy on my hip. I was trying to frost a cake and had called Scott for a consultation about the texture of the frosting. But like usual, the conversation moved into a discussion about Miss Lewis and, then, about our families.

"Your family can never really see you," he said. "No matter how much you want them to, they just will never see the whole person. They can't. They just can't. And there is no way for us to see our families that way."

And then it struck me. I could wish for the rest of my life that my family might see me the way I see myself, but they never will. They love all of me, of course. But they can only ever see me as a sister or a daughter. That's how it is for everyone, and that's why we go outside to create new families.

Someone told me once that the blessing is often next to the wound. For kids like Scott and me who grew up gay, that pain of rejection, of not being seen, of knowing your parents don't understand or might even hate a most essential part of you, is a wound. But that pain can also give you the freedom to walk outside of the constraints of family, and of society. It's instant permission to create a new kind of family. I did that with Katia and Sammy. And in making my new family, I could finally make peace with my old one.

On a recent Valentine's Day, my mother called to read a card my father had given her. Fifty-four years of marriage, and he pulled a beauty out of the drugstore bin. It spoke of how she was the love of his life, and how each trial and hardship he watched her go through only made her more beautiful to him.

"Oh, honey," she said to me when she was done reading it out loud. "Isn't that the sweetest thing you have ever heard?"

I was standing on a beach with Katia and the baby, three thousand miles away.

"I hope my relationship can be as strong as yours one day, Mom," I said.

"Well, I'm sure it will be," she said. "You wish Katia and the baby a happy Valentine's Day from us."

I asked Scott for a recipe that reflected the family he made with Miss Lewis. He gave me this one, a simple pan cornbread they made together many nights. They loved it with soft butter and honey.

OUR FAVORITE SOUR CORNBREAD

1½ cups fine-ground white cornmeal

1 teaspoon salt

1 teaspoon baking powder (Scott and Edna always used homemade baking

powder, which they made by sifting together ¼ cup cream of tartar
with 2 tablespoons baking soda)

1¾ cups buttermilk or, in a pinch, 1¾ cups milk curdled by adding 2
teaspoons lemon juice and 2 teaspoons cider vinegar

2 eggs, lightly beaten

2 tablespoons unsalted butter

1. Preheat oven to 450 degrees.
2. Mix together the cornmeal, salt and baking powder in
   a bowl.
3. Stir the buttermilk into the beaten eggs, and pour over the
   dry ingredients in batches, stirring vigorously to make a
   smooth, glossy batter.
4. Cut the butter into pieces and put it in a 10-inch cast-iron
   skillet or baking pan. Put the skillet in the preheated oven
   and heat until the butter is melted and foaming. Remove
   from the oven and swirl the butter in the skillet to coat the
   bottoms and sides thoroughly.
5. Pour the extra melted butter from the pan into the
   cornbread batter and stir well until the butter is absorbed
   into the batter.
6. Turn the batter into the heated skillet and put it in the oven
   to bake for 30 to 40 minutes, until the cornbread is golden
   brown and crusty on top and pulls away from the sides of
   the skillet.
7. Remove the skillet from the oven and turn the cornbread
   out onto a plate. Allow to cool for five minutes before
   cutting into wedges. Serve the cornbread hot.

8

How Cool Is That?

Rural Wisconsin can be grim in November. It's worse if you go there for a funeral. Outside the window of our rental car, silos and cows and barns slipped by. Leafless trees jutted into a sky the color of wet cement. The dim winter light of the Rust Belt made afternoon seem like twilight.

I wasn't supposed to be in this Buick with my parents, driving from the Minneapolis airport north to Cumberland, a lake town of 2,800 people where my mother grew up. I was supposed to be sitting at dinner with Rachael Ray in a charming little restaurant she likes in the West Village, living my fabulous life.

We were driving to Cumberland because my godmother had died. It had been a long march to the end. Phillomena Zappa De-Gidio was eighty-three. She had Parkinson's, just like my mom does. In this part of northern Wisconsin, so many people have Parkinson's they call it Italian sickle cell. My mother was in a study about siblings with Parkinson's, but no one knows for sure if there is a genetic link or if maybe all those agricultural chemicals caused it. My cousins and I all worry that we're next, but so far no one has had the money or the courage to get tested. For the moment, I just don't want to know that much about my future.

When the call about my aunt came, my parents were in Carmel Valley, California, celebrating Thanksgiving with my oldest brother, Keith. There was no time to head back to their home in Colorado, so they just got on a plane bound for the Midwest with whatever outerwear and funeral clothes they could piece together. I threw a black suit and some long underwear in a suitcase and headed to LaGuardia with a ticket Katia found for me online.

My mother was already starting to slow down a little from the disease, and traveling was getting harder for her. When I met her at the Minneapolis airport, she had only a thin red coat wrapped tightly around her. It wasn't much defense against the cold that was already seeping into our bones.

"Oh, Mom," I said, pulling her against me to try to warm her up. "I'm so sorry."

"I am too, honey," she said.

I couldn't imagine how this was going to be for her. My mom was the second youngest in a family of eleven children. Aunt Phil was one of the oldest. In many ways, her sister was like a mother to her. Attending her funeral, and knowing she died from complications brought on by the same disease Mom had, was going to be nothing but grueling. There was no question that I would make the trip. I wanted to honor my aunt but also to help my mother. I was old enough now and I had lived enough life to understand what my job as the eldest daughter was. There just comes a point where you realize it is time to show up for your parents, no matter what has passed between you or how you were raised or how busy you are. You just have to show up.

We piled into the car and left Minneapolis. After a couple of hours, we pulled into little ol' Cumberland. The town has a few defining characteristics. For one thing, it's home to some of the best Italian sausages I have ever had. They make them at a place called Louie's Finer Meats, where the butchers also sell summer sausage that has been molded into the shape of a beer bottle. Cumberland is the site of the annual Rutabaga Fest, held every August. They fry up a kind of thin-skinned Italian pepper that I can never seem to find anywhere else. A scoop goes onto a patty of Italian sausage that's been cooked like a hamburger. It's all served on a bun soft enough to take up the juice but still sturdy enough to hold everything together.

Back in the day, my mother was the Rutabaga Princess. She was a striking young woman, my mother. And the first Italian to hold the title, people say. With the exception of a small group of Native Americans, Cumberland is a white place. For years, the social division was between the Italians and everyone else—mostly people whose roots were Nordic or Germanic. The Italians were on the bottom rungs of the social ladder.

"They would call us names like greasy dago, sometimes," she told me. This makes her victory as the Rutabaga Princess all the more special. And it's probably the reason my mother has always been a big defender of the underdog in any given situation.

In the fall and winter, there's not much going on for a visitor who doesn't deer hunt or ice fish. For kicks, relatives will drive you forty-five minutes down the road to the Indian casino at Turtle Lake or maybe take you for a spin past the Packer House. It's a modest split-level painted entirely in the green and gold of the Green Bay Packers, right down to the half-barrel barbecue grill on the back porch.

There is a special Italian cemetery in Cumberland, right across the parking lot from St. Anthony Abbot Church, which my grandfather John Zappa helped build. If you walk through the first few rows, you will see weathered white tombstones bearing faded cameo photographs of my grandfather and my grandmother Florence Ranallo Zappa. We drove by it on the way to my cousin's house, and my mom piped up.

"Grandpa bought that whole section so we could all be together," she said.

But she won't be buried there. Only half of her ten brothers and sisters will be. The rest, like my mom, left the dairy farm they grew up on and started families in other towns. They had a longing to move up and out, to be something bigger than they were born to. It's a desire that got passed on to me.

As we drive through the town, I feel so much a part of the place but also like a complete stranger. I don't know this town, really, but I feel like I'm related to everyone in it. My godmother, Aunt Phil, was the matriarch of the Zappa sisters, the one whose red sauce was the sauce to emulate. She and her husband, Louie, had owned a restaurant called the Tower House. They sold it years ago and bought a shoe store. When we were kids, we visited Cumberland on summer vacation. Once, we got to run through the store and pick out any shoes we wanted. I selected moccasins with tiny turquoise beads sewn over the toes in some kind of pattern meant to look vaguely Native American.

Our branch of the family was never as tight a part of the Zappa clan as those siblings who stayed in Cumberland. Even when we caught sunfish and jumped in the lake outside my Aunt Phil's house, or helped make the little tightly rolled pasta called cavatelli and sweet, hot pizza frite, we were never quite a part of it all. We had moved on to cities they had never visited. Even when I spent a couple of weeks there one summer with my cousins, drinking strawberry wine and trying to act older than I was, I felt like the goofy teenage outcast from the suburbs. But it was one of the best memories of my early adolescence. Later, when I was older, I went back and told my cousins how much that summer meant to me. They didn't remember it at all. Funny thing, memory.

Still, I always liked going back to the farmhouse where my mother grew up. I couldn't get enough of it, peering into the room that seemed too small for her to have shared with so many other girls and imagining what the kitchen used to be like before it had modern appliances. I would make her walk me around on a narrated tour of her childhood while my dad drank ginger brandy at the kitchen table with the uncles who still worked the farm.

The older I got, the more I came to see how I inherited not only the kind of genes that might one day give me Parkinson's but also the kind that come from immigrants who had nothing more than the land they farmed. A need to keep working toward something better is in my bones. There's always more work to do, right? There is perhaps no better example of that than my Aunt Phil.

The funeral was pretty much all set before she died. That's because Aunt Phil was the toughest, hardest-working auntie I had. Her daughter, Sharon, is the same way. That family is so organized that they had long ago arranged every last detail of the funeral meal that would be served across the street from St. Anthony's at the Knights of Columbus community hall. The ladies from the church make the funeral sauce and serve it over mostacolli in big enameled roasting pans. They toss a simple green salad with oil and vinegar. If you paid extra, like my aunt did, you could get Italian sausage instead of the luncheon ham. "I don't want any of that slimy ham," she said more than once.

After the funeral, my uncle Louie gave me her copy of the St.

Anthony's community cookbook. I cherish it. As community cook-books go, it's a real gem, with recipes for scarzel, which is an Easter bread stuffed with farmer's cheese and raisins, and a recipe for the famous funeral sauce. But my favorite is for something simply called "Jewish muffins." They are made from a batter thick with oats and nuts. It must have been a contribution from the lone Jewish family that somewhere along the line became one of the Frozen Chosen in the great deer hunting country of northern Wisconsin.

When we showed up at Sharon's house that day, I saw how different we were, my country mouse cousin and the city mouse me. But we were also exactly the same. Sharon and I were both working hard, trying to move ahead. And we just wanted to do right by our mothers. Sharon had been the one to take care of her mom in those hard last years. I knew that when the time came and I had to take care of mine, Sharon would tell me how to do it. She would be the only one who would understand the pain that would surely come, and why the burden would fall to the daughters in ways it would never fall on the sons.

Once we settled in around a big kitchen table that held bowls of roasted Italian sausage and ashtrays and cups of coffee, I decided to make a move. Maybe cheer things up a little.

"I have a message for you, Sharon," I said. "It's from my friend Rachael Ray."

She was incredulous.

"You know Rachael Ray?"

Sure, I said. I had written a story about her for the *Times* a month or so ago. In fact, I was just going to have dinner with her. This is the message she left when I called to cancel because I had to come here, I explained.

I play her the recording. It's sweet and animated and sincere. "I am so sorry about your Aunt Phillomena!" Rachael says. "Tell your family Rach sends her condolences."

Each time it ends, I hit a button and pass it to the next person. It's a party trick, and I supplement it with stories about other famous people I have met. But all the while, I am thinking in the back of my head, You are a complete jackass. They are all onto you.

I'm not going to lie to you here. For as much as I eventually came to identify with Rachael and her work ethic, for as much as I was intellectually fascinated with her story, part of the attraction was watching her fame explode. I mean, who doesn't like to feel a little close to a celebrity? Just the hint that someone famous was in the same room, ate at the same table or may have touched the very same doorknob perks people up. Those of us who traffic in the ordinary love to hear about famous people. Even at the *Times*, where many reporters have regular contact with celebrity, this disease is pervasive. I have watched very smart critics walk down the same hall three or four times because a minor celeb like George Hamilton was getting interviewed in a glass-walled conference room. (I only walked by once.)

Most of us have a few random celebrity encounters we like to brag about. I have stood next to the actor Steve Buscemi to buy a bagel. I have had brunch at Jessica Lange's sister's house. But I have also had plenty that were directly related to my job. I have met more famous chefs than anyone should have to. I have even ridden in the back of Joanne Woodward's Prius while she and Paul Newman drove me back to the train station after we had dinner. When I asked him how the car handled, thinking this would be a good way to small-talk a race car driver, he started swerving all over the road. Ha, ha! That was a good one, Paul.

When I find myself meeting a celebrity or just accidentally standing next to one (which oddly happens a lot in New York), I say what my oldest brother, Keith, the most polite man in the universe, taught me to say: "I really appreciate your work." Then I spend the rest of the day telling people I stood next to someone famous. Sometimes, I think this makes me a terrible, shallow person. I'm not proud that I sometimes think being around someone famous means something special is happening, and that I, too, am a little bit special. But then the inevitable happens. It usually turns out the famous person is not all that special. The famous person is flawed. It's like finally seeing a picture of someone you listen to a lot on the radio. It ruins everything. And no matter how famous the person is whom you meet, you always have to go back to being your old, average self.

Ever since that day at my cousin's, I have thought a lot about why I played that message from Rachael over and over. Initially, my intention was to bring a little light to a dark time. To entertain and play the clown. But really, I think I was trying to be something I wasn't. I was trying to be a big shot who knew famous people.

A few years later, I came across one of those Internet accountings of the characteristics of different cities and towns. The ones that start, "You know you're from X if Y . . ." It went like this:

You know you're from Cumberland if you've ever . . .

driven a tractor to school.

kept score by hand when you go bowling.

owned a deer camp.

ridden a snowmobile to the Dairy Queen.

This is the truth about me and my people. I can go to all the fancy dinners I want and collect celebrity friends and journalism awards, but I am a girl predisposed to riding a snowmobile to the Dairy Queen.

I am the daughter of a woman who grew up on a dairy farm and a man who lived in a basement until his father could build a house on top of it. I am not a Detroit street tough, as I once wished I was, or a wealthy East Coaster with a fancy degree, which I used to think came with the keys to the kingdom.

I have a state school education, a drinking problem and I like girls, not boys. I don't tan well, and I'm always about fifteen pounds too heavy. I'm not so great with money and I sometimes act before I think. But I'm also (most days) a helpful citizen of the world. I've got a good sense of humor and a decent softball arm. And I have gotten pretty good at being a daughter, a wife, a friend and, lately, a mother.

In other words, I'm me.

After that funeral, it would take another few years to finally real-ize that trying to be something I'm not wasn't going to get me any-where except miserable. And spending a little time close to the tornado that is Rachael Ray helped me understand the value of authenticity. The most valuable thing I have is who I am.

Rachael Domenica Ray, small-town cheerleader turned cooking rock star, and I, Wisconsin dairy queen turned writer, share a couple of essential traits. One is that we are inclined, out of fear as much as ambition, to work hard. The other is that we are who we are largely because of our mothers.

An Italian daughter and her mother have a special bond. The sons might be the princes, but the daughters are the ones who will suffer for their mother in ways the boys will never know. We take the brunt, and we get the rewards. But mostly, we work our asses off to live up to our mothers. Because, at least in my case and Rachael's, we live under the idea that our mothers worked much harder than we did, that we will never be good enough and that without them we will be lost.

Pleasing your mother becomes a maddening art form for Italian daughters. It can feed a drive that ends up producing some pretty good results, but it also produces a kind of over-reliance on ambition. It can set a girl up for a lifetime of trying to be something other than exactly who you are. And that is one of my key character defects.

Just about the time I was really in the middle of the scrum in New York, trying to fit in at the *Times* and make my way through a city where ambition runs through the gutters, I decided I wanted to know more about Rachael Ray. Say what you will about her food style, her love of the phrase "yum-o" or her thirty-minute shtick, Rachael has led back to the kitchen a whole generation for whom *The Joy of Cooking* might as well be the Koran and the drive-through lane the family dinner table.

Other women whom I admire for their cooking skills and their dedication to keeping us all at the table might not like that Rachael is among my teachers. But she is really the bridge between someone like, say, Marion Cunningham and people in their twenties and thirties who are as comfortable cooking as they are texting. I don't think Rachael planned to be such a big part of America's move back to the kitchen, but I do think she knew instinctively that people missed cooking for each other, and they were longing for real food. The best part is that she is unapologetic about her own culinary skills and her reliance on shortcuts.

"I have no formal anything," she said. "I'm completely unqualified for any job I've ever had."

Once her popularity grew, the mix of making money while helping people out could not have been a more powerful elixir. But writing about her would be a challenge. *The New York Times* Dining section generally doesn't traffic in the comings and goings of Food Network stars. Using sheer numbers alone, I made a case that she was the most influential woman cooking today. Rachael has more than a dozen cookbooks and is on her way to having six million books in print. At one point, five of them were on my newspaper's bestseller list at once. She has done three Food Network shows and runs a monthly magazine, *Every Day with Rachael Ray.* She sells a line of knives, pans and appliances and has bottled her own brand of extra-virgin olive oil (EVOO) and chicken stock. But her biggest hit comes from her daily talk show. About 2.6 million people watch it every day. It was created in tandem with Oprah Winfrey's people and King World Productions.

"You've got a great personality," Ms. Winfrey said when Rachael appeared on her show back before the magazine or the television show began. "That's why you're such a hit. People like you."

I can see now that one of the reasons I was so taken with Rachael is that she is exactly who she is, on and off camera. She is, in a word, authentic. I had been at the *Times* and in New York for a year, but I was still working up the courage to just be who I was. New York is a city that thrives as much on image as grit, but I felt neither flashy enough nor gritty enough to be at home. But I was getting better at it. At home, Katia and I were crazy happy. She was showing me her New York, the one where you hang out in the cool apartments of great friends and get season tickets to the Public Theater and take the subway to whole new worlds. We were jumping into our car or on a plane whenever we wanted to see family and explore parts of the East Coast that were new to us.

During long days at work, getting back to our brownstone at night was my carrot. If I could just survive the daily swim in my own sea of insecurity at the office, I knew I would find solace at home where someone knew me—all of me—and loved me anyway. And we were starting to talk about how to have a child. I was convinced I was too old to conceive without a lot of medical intervention, something I was not interested in enduring. That left one womb in the house. So we began the long process of saving money and figuring out who would donate the sperm and getting all our legal paperwork together so we could make a family.

In the meantime, I was starting to get my sea legs at work. I decided to push to write the stories that I was interested in, not ones the editors dreamed up. I had to not care if my colleagues thought the loud girl in sensible shoes who didn't speak French and had only a vague working knowledge of New York restaurant history was cheapening the franchise. So one day, I bounded up to an editor's desk like a golden retriever.

"How about a profile of Rachael Ray?" I asked.

"She's not a good cook," the editor sniffed.

I understood the concern. The subject of a *Times* Dining story needs to have a certain level of culinary prowess. And a profile of a cook usually involves recipes. The recipes, generally, need to tell a story or offer a new technique. Sometimes they might offer quick ways around more laborious tasks, but not at the expense of flavor or quality of ingredients. To shorthand it, we will never use pre-shredded cheese from a bag or suggest that store-bought ice cream covered with fudge sauce, cayenne pepper and Grand Marnier is a suitable dessert. But those are the kinds of things on which Rachael's entire culinary canon is built. Let the big-name chefs fuss with foams and sous-vide. She'll stick with hot dog nachos and "jambalika," a dish that is kind of like jambalaya. Prepared biscuit dough, frozen corn and pre-bagged greens are the coin of her realm.

To be fair, though, some of Rachael's food is really worth eating. She starts with quality olive oil (often her own brand) and uses good, solid cooking technique. There are some surprisingly great dishes under those cute names. But her recipes are easy to mock. She invents things like beer margaritas, stoup (a cross between a soup and a stew) and paella burgers. The latter is her big, sloppy homage to the Spanish dish, built with a ground-chicken patty, grilled linguiça and butterflied shrimp stacked with shredded lettuce on a big Portuguese roll. On her show, Rachael tried to lift the greasy behemoth to her mouth and declared: "Look at that. It's the size of my head!"

Rachael is a regular target of chefs and food bloggers. Someone even developed a drinking game around her cutesy-pie catchphrases—EVOO, delish, sammies and the like. Players take a sip when she uses one on TV. If she creates a new and completely unnecessary abbreviation, they have to swallow the whole drink. "This is awesome," she said when I showed her the list. "But man, people are going to get hammered."

To those and her other critics, I say consider that the woman writes recipes more frequently than you brush your teeth. Every day, she has to produce something, and she is always scrambling for a new idea. That's pressure, my friends. Her method isn't fancy. She just scribbles in a notebook. Sometimes, her recipes come from dishes she tastes as she travels, which she does a lot. She throws it all in that inexpensive little notebook and then finds a way to turn those ideas into something she can use. She is always tossing out ideas and producing recipes that might go in a new book or her magazine or on one of her television shows. It's like those people who have to wash their hands fourteen times before they can leave the house, only with her it's about scribbling ideas. On camera, she delivers them effortlessly with a charisma that is as God-given as a star pitcher's right arm. More than one of the people she works with calls her a machine, which is another reason I liked her. We both understood from an early age that the only way we were going to survive was to work hard.

My story about her came out just before her magazine and her talk show debuted. It was before her wave crested, before she got really, really famous. Like the kind of famous that has millions of dollars attached to it and lands your face on the cover of the tabloids every time you fight with your husband in public. After it was published, Rachael and I kept in touch. I watched her tape a show with President Clinton as a guest, and listened to her husband's band. She sent us cute T-shirts when our daughter, Sammy, was born. They had slogans like Grilled Cheese Sammy. Rachael calls sandwiches Sammies. Get it? Rachael says she's going to have one made up that says "Club Sammy" when my girl turns thirteen.

Sometimes I'd eat with her and her husband, John, and their dog Isaboo in her cute, comfortable multilevel apartment on a side street in Greenwich Village. It's got a small kitchen and a deck and a big dining table. Rachael and John are happy to show it off, gushing over a bathroom improvement or a huge grill that needed a crane to move it onto the roof. They bought the apartment because it has short little staircases connecting the levels and Rachael's beloved first dog, Boo, was getting old and couldn't climb a lot of stairs at once. That dog's death was one of the worst days of her life. She'll tell you about that kind of grief, her bathroom remodel and how weird some of the stars she interviews are all in the same conversation and somehow make them all seem connected. She'll do it with a glass of wine in one hand and a spatula in the other. When she's in her apartment, she's all about movies and jousting with her husband and entertaining a few friends and ignoring the messy kitchen floor. When she's in yours, she'll be the first one to jump up and do the dishes.

This is the thing that attracted me to her the most. Excepting the fact that she is enormously famous and rich, she really is just like your neighbor, or your brother's girlfriend, or, maybe, you. And she loves her mother, just like I do. "If anything," Rachael said, "I'm a poor knockoff of her."

I first met Elsa Scuderi in a little cabin near Lake Luzerne in upstate New York. I drove five hours from Brooklyn, winding my car down a little road until I came upon a garden that was entirely out of place among the little cabins around it. Although Rachael owns it and visits regularly, her mother lives in one of the cabins most of the time, driving around town in the new Mini Cooper her daughter bought her, and decorating the place and the grounds around it. "It looks like the garden of Versailles," Rachael points out.

Paved stone paths wind around fire pits, benches and a bocce court. Her mother's little workshop in a shed near the cabin is nicer than a lot of New York apartments. "This is what happens once a person retires and they've worked all their life and you leave them alone in the woods," Elsa said.

I made the drive while I was still researching my story. Rachael loves to talk on the phone, and I had already spent hours on the calls, doing household chores with the phone headset on, taking a few notes and even flopping back on my bed during some of them. "New York Times chick" is how she started referring to me, and at some point she decided it would be OK to invite me to her little sanctuary upstate. The cabin and the mother within it are Rachael's touchstones.

For dinner, she made her go-to fall dish: penne with sweet Italian sausage, canned pumpkin and sage. Like all Rachael's dishes, it's about ease and speed but with aspirations to be something more than it is. You brown some Italian sausage, and then sauté garlic and onion. Deglaze the pan with some white wine, add chicken stock and stir in the canned pumpkin with a little cinnamon and nutmeg. Toss all that with Parmesan and chopped fresh sage. Boom. Dinner.

She spent a lot more time talking than cooking. She's a great talker, and always in motion. So it was no surprise that she cut a nice gash in her thumb. She bandaged it up, laughed it off and kept chopping.

Most of the thousands of recipes Rachael has "canoodled" over the years were written in her cabin. She had rented what she called "this crappy house" in the early 1990s, before it all happened, and has lived there off and on with her mother and, sometimes, her younger brother, since. Some months, she could barely put together enough money to cover the $550 rent.

"It was check-to-check living," she said. "I would go buy groceries and you know when you swipe your bank card thing? I would get so nervous the bank card would be declined. It makes you so sick you want to throw up."

When she got out of high school, she stuck around Lake George, but the cycle of small-town life and low-paying jobs was wearing thin. In 1995, she headed to New York City. She worked first at the Macy's Marketplace candy counter and moved up the ranks quickly, learning about everything from buying cheese to how to shop for Liza Minnelli's holiday food gifts. When Macy's tried to promote her to a buyer in accessories, she moved to Agata & Valentina, the specialty foods store.

She stayed in the city for only two years, getting dragged down by the grind of it. She had a bad breakup, then a broken ankle. Then she got mugged in front of her apartment in Queens. She Maced him, but the guy was so mad he came back the next weekend, dragged her down an alley and beat her up with his gun. That was enough. She left New York and moved back into the cabin.

Rachael eventually landed a job at the fanciest food and equipment store in Albany. She was a buyer and a cook, preparing hundreds of pounds of food every day. As a holiday promotion, she developed a class to help people get dinner on the table in half an hour. It caught on, and she started teaching the concept at a chain of local grocery stores. The beginning of her media break came when a reporter from a Schenectady television station called. He was looking to do a story about gourmet doughnuts, a short-lived trend in the early 1990s when Krispy Kreme had its moment. The store wasn't selling fancy doughnuts, but Rachael plowed ahead. She told him she could show him how to slap a meal together fast.

"I can't boil water," the reporter told her.

"Yes, you can," she told him. "Come to one of my cooking classes and I can teach you to cook dinner in thirty minutes or less."

He did, and the segment was a hit. She ended up being a regular on the station. She continued perfecting her thirty-minute meal concept, eventually schlepping a little demo cart around every Price Chopper she could get into in upstate New York. Soon, she figured she could sell a cookbook, so she talked a tiny independent Manhattan publishing company into turning her pile of photocopied recipes into *30-Minute Meals*.

A Food Network executive heard Rachael cook on an upstate public radio show in 2001. About the same time, a *Today* show producer saw her book and, with some prodding from Al Roker, who was also from upstate, called and asked her to appear. Her hard work was about to pay off. The night before she was to go on, it started to snow. When storms hit upstate New York, snow is measured in feet. But this was the moment, so Rachael and her mom drove nine hours south through the storm. She nailed the *Today* show appearance. Not too much later, she met with Food Network executives, who signed her to a $360,000 contract.

The first thing she did was to reupholster the old family furniture in the cabin. Then she bought the place. But she had no clue about the money. "I kept all of my money my first year in my checking account," she said. "It didn't occur to me to do anything else with it."

Rachael credits luck for her big break, but really she had been working toward it her whole life. She was born precocious, and always had the idea that if she just tried hard enough, things would happen. As a teenager, she wrote a letter to John Peterman because she loved the J. Peterman catalog and had some thoughts she wanted to share. She wrote "Little Girl, Big Ideas" at the top of the page. A couple of years later, she wrote to Harry Connick Sr., then the New Orleans district attorney, proposing he send his son north to a jazz

supper club she wanted to open in Saratoga Springs. The two became pen pals.

Her first business was a gift basket service called Delicious Liai-
sons. She was still in high school. While other people were out
partying, she would spend evenings in her room, putting together
baskets of pasta and cocoa mix and hand-lettering her catalog. She
was industrious, albeit a pain in the ass sometimes. These are traits
I entirely relate to.

"You were always busy, always organized," my mother told me
during the many conversations where I would try to get her to describe what I was like as a child.

How, I'd ask? Do you remember anything specific?

"Oh, I don't know," she'd say, "just busy."

I grew up around people who worked hard. I can recall only one
or two days when my father wasn't working, and those were because
he was so sick he couldn't get out of bed. Aside from the occasional
nap in front of a soap opera when a day was just too long, my
mother was in constant motion, just like Aunt Phil.

Rachael grew up around hard work, too. First it was her grandfather, an Italian immigrant and a stonecutter who instilled in
Rachael's mother and in her both a love of food and an appreciation of a hard day's work. He was the family's main cook, and he
grew and prepared almost everything for his family of twelve. Her
father's side of the family was skilled in Louisiana cooking. The Ray
family owned four restaurants in Cape Cod. When she was eight
years old, the family relocated to upstate New York. Rachael's parents were finally divorced when she was thirteen. Her father, whom
Rachael has repeatedly had to tell to stop talking to the tabloids,
lives in Saratoga Springs. She doesn't talk to him much. Upstate,
her mother made do as a single parent of three. She helped manage

a string of upstate restaurants, and Rachael was forever filling in for absent dishwashers and waitresses. Her mother, who used to pin McGovern buttons to her children's clothes, turned Rachael into a political junkie and a news freak.

"I loved 60 *Minutes*," she said. "I had a thing for Harry Reasoner. I just loved Hugh Downs." Tony Bennett came to her house for dinner after she got famous and gave her advice on how to manage her voice. She told me she has a soft spot for older men.

Her mother made sure the children got to New York City, that they had a taste of something bigger. My mother did the same for us. We weren't going to the opera, but we ate out at good restaurants, spent all day at the library and joined every sports team that came along. We played instruments. She even tried to see if I liked ballet. And just to make sure we understood gratitude, she'd haul us along to clean halfway houses or fill grocery bags with donated food. My mother was nothing if not the quintessential volunteer and helper of the less fortunate.

This is another point at which Rachael and I intersect. No matter how big she gets, Rachael always seems to feel like she's not doing enough for people. Her mother used to carry around a list of people and organizations Rachael had given money to so she would feel better about saying no. She eventually set up a foundation called Yum-O so she could target her charitable work toward improving kids' health through eating and exercise. Former president Bill Clinton's Alliance for a Healthier Generation is her partner.

Her mother also sorts through some fan mail, which can range from children's drawings to marriage proposals to letters from recently widowed senior citizens. "She's big with the guys, let me tell you," her mother said.

Her mom also counsels Rachael on her marriage to John Cusimano, a lawyer and a guitar player in a band called The Cringe. He is also her business partner and lawyer. She met him at a party in 2001. A friend had invited her specifically to fix her up with someone. Rachael was not so into the matchmaking, but she went anyway, on the promise that there would be no yenta action. She saw John. They were the only two short people in the room.

"It was like a stupid movie. We locked eyes and crossed the room toward each other," she said. They started talking, and Rachael asked him what she usually asks guys: What do you like to cook? "They always say chicken or chili," she explained.

But not John. "Tilapia was on sale so I sautéed it and made a nice tomato sauce and deglazed the pan with some Negra Modelo beer and sliced some avocado," he told her.

"Oh, you're gay! I have to set you up with some of my friends."

"Uh, no," he said.

"Then I got it," she told me. "I was like, ding ding ding!"

Later that night, the woman who invited her to the party pulled her aside. "That's the guy I tried to introduce you to," she said.

"We were together on the phone or in person together every day since," Rachael said.

It is a famously volatile relationship but a damn sweet one, too. "They're just Italian," says a friend, explaining away the verbal fireworks.

Her mother worries that Rachael pushes herself too hard, but then again she's got hundreds of people whose jobs depend on simply what's coming out of her head. She runs it like it is all going to go away tomorrow, and she is making a grab for the cash. It's not in a greedy way, exactly. It's more like someone who never had a lot money might.

"I think she's one of those for-the-moment people," said someone who works with her. "She's opportunistic. I don't think she'll sell her soul to the devil, but I think she sees opportunity and goes for it. She's always thinking money."

Rachael recognizes that money is how some people keep score. She knows class matters, but it shouldn't. "I love breaking down those walls between the haves and have-nots," Rachael said.

I don't doubt it's out of caring, but I suspect that much of her openheartedness comes out of a need to be liked. This is another trait we share. We both need to make people happy. It's linked to the fear that if we stop pushing, even for a minute, everything will go away. We will be left alone. Or—and maybe this is worse—we won't make our moms happy and keep them safe.

"I'm such a pleaser," she said. "I'm such a waitress."

So how do you help people out, how do you honor your authentically generous nature, and not get it all tangled up in your own shit? I asked Rachael that once. Just knowing it made a difference, she said. Just being aware of the tendency.

"That takes the pressure off," she said. But she didn't want to go much deeper, to go over it a million times, like I tend to.

"I've just never had the time or money to go to shrinks. They always scared me," she said. "I always thought of them as scab pickers. Just let it heal."

Me, I needed the therapy. Over the years, I probably spent a couple of years' worth of rent on it. And I have spent a lifetime on the phone with my sober friends and my family kicking around my problems. I've spent a lot of time listening to theirs, too. And I figured this much out. You can find God, make as much money as God or be as good-looking as God, and you'll still need to figure out a way to unpack the emotional baggage you were handed when you were a kid. Like needing to please people. Or thinking you weren't good enough.

After I stopped drinking, my character defects got illuminated big on the walls. Without a little booze and maybe some narcotics to make them again invisible, they had to be dealt with or they were too much to bear. If I didn't untangle it all, soon I'd be deciding that a vodka-flavored drink would be a far better idea than, say, continuing my efforts to be patient, helpful and to leave other people's business alone.

I found a mirror of sorts in Rachael. And I got to witness, even just a little bit, what unbridled ambition can do to someone.

Rachael lives a life bigger than I want. I can't afford it emotionally, even though these days, my character defects could maybe fit in something the size of a rolling suitcase. I am aiming for a carry-on bag one day, then maybe a lunch sack. With luck and diligence, one day they'll fit in a pocket. But I have no illusions that I won't struggle with them until the day I die.

A nagging one is the struggle with ambition. If you ask me, I'll tell you that I don't think I am all that ambitious—just terrified of going back to the place where I couldn't pay the bills and suicide seemed a viable option. Really, I tell my friends, I'd prefer a simple life with Katia, babies and some goats. I didn't plan to have a big life and work at a place where the stakes are high and the pressure gets more intense the more one seems to succeed. Can't people see that I really believe that line of Lily Tomlin's—the one where she says even if you win the rat race you're still a rat?

My friends just laugh at me when I start talking about this. And I suppose it's true. As much as I want to get out of the rat race, I still want to be the best rat. I want to be the best little recipe writer ever. Because I think, on some level, that I am a fraud. And if I just get the right trophy or job or girlfriend or bank account or haircut or jeans, then everything will be OK. I will be able to stop running. I will be just fine, exactly as I am. I will be seen for who I am, and it will be enough.

What I'm coming to understand is that my mother, my friends and the world will like me just fine even if I don't know anyone famous, if I don't do a good job or if I don't succeed. And if they don't, well, I'll still be OK. I am the strongest when I am my authentic self. Anytime I try to be something I'm not, to pretend I've read a book I haven't or that I'm a celebrity because I have met a few and have their voices on my phone, I get into trouble.

I need to keep it as real as I can. Because now, there's another life involved. If I have learned anything, it's that mothers influence their daughters. And already, my daughter not even out of diapers, I can see how my likes and dislikes influence her. I can see how my unending love of going places and seeing friends and laughing as hard as I can is rubbing off. People say she is the most social baby they've ever met.

I want her to know the value of hard work, sure. And of giving to others. I want her to know that her mom is just a girl inclined to ride to the Dairy Queen on a snowmobile. And I want her to be herself.

———

Rachael has a real fondness for eggplant. So did my Aunt Phil. And since they are both stars to me, I offer modified versions of both their recipes. The difference in how the two are written is striking. Rachael's represents the new reality in cooking. That is, people need a lot of very basic instructions. The other one, which my brother Kent recorded from my mother, who got it from my cousin, represents a more old-fashioned form of recipe sharing—one that assumes a lot of cooking knowledge, as well as some family history.

RACHAEL RAY'S FAMILY CAPONATA

> 3 tablespoons EVOO (*her shorthand for extra-virgin olive oil*)
>
> 4 cloves garlic, chopped
>
> ½–¾ teaspoon crushed red pepper flakes
>
> 1 red bell pepper, seeded and diced
>
> 1 cubanelle pepper (long, green Italian pepper), seeded and diced
>
> 1 large sweet onion, peeled and chopped
>
> 2 ribs celery, chopped
>
> ½ cup large green olives, pitted and chopped
>
> ½ cup black kalamata olives, pitted and chopped
>
> 1 jar capers (3 ounces), drained
>
> ½ cup golden raisins (a couple of handfuls)
>
> 1 medium firm eggplant, diced
>
> Salt
>
> 1 can diced tomatoes (32 ounces)

1 can crushed tomatoes (14 ounces)
¼ cup flat-leaf parsley, chopped (a handful)

1. Preheat a deep pot over medium heat. Add olive oil, about three turns of the pan, garlic and crushed pepper.
2. Add the vegetables (peppers, onion and celery) to the pot as you go.
3. Once vegetables are all in, increase heat to medium-high. Stir in olives, capers and raisins. Salt the diced eggplant and stir into the pot.
4. Add tomatoes, both diced and crushed, and stir well to combine. Cover pot and cook caponata 15 to 20 minutes, until vegetables are tender. Stir in parsley and remove pan from heat. Let stand a few minutes or chill before serving. For a main dish, you can also toss this with pasta, a little more oil and pecorino cheese.

AUNT PHIL'S MELANZANE, WITH A TINY VARIATION

Eggplant
Salt
Hot fresh peppers
Garlic
Vinegar
Olive oil

1. Peel eggplant and slice thin, salt and let it sit overnight.
2. Put in a press and squeeze out all the moisture. (Use two

plates weighted with a can, or put the slices in a colander with towels on top and then a can on top of the towels. Or, like my brother, use an old necktie press.)

3. Slice the hot peppers and garlic thin.
4. Boil the vinegar and blanch each slice of eggplant in the hot liquid for about 10 seconds.
5. Pack in layers in pint ring-top jars and fill with olive oil.

NOTE: You can eat the melanzane in a day or two. Or you can preserve it by using the cold-pack canning method.

■ 9 ■

What's Done Is Done

The first cookbook my mother ever gave me was *The Classic
Italian Cook Book*. It was also the first one Marcella Hazan
ever wrote.

My mother took a blue ballpoint pen and, on the inside of the
front cover, wrote: "To Kimmie, who cooks from the heart—love
you, Mommie."

That was in 1984. I was twenty-three years old, a wild young
adult with one foot barely out of college and another suspended,
midair, waiting to land on whatever was coming next. I had no idea
that decades later, that book would lead me to the most important
lesson of all.

When the book came in the mail, I had just moved to Seattle to
try to start what would be another failed relationship and to begin
my professional life. It hadn't started with much promise. I was
handing out towels at a YMCA by day and proofreading an alterna-
tive weekly by night.

My mother and I were just barely beginning to learn how to see
each other as women instead of mother and daughter. We weren't
very good at it. We were still too afraid to really tell each other the

truth about anything. She hadn't stopped needing to change me, and I had not stopped needing to be changed. She still wanted to love me in a certain way, and I wanted to be loved in a different way. Too many phone conversations still ended in arguments with her telling me what I should be doing and me hanging up like a child who didn't get her way. We hadn't figured out the unconditional part.

At the time, I was completely unsure about who I was and still wholly, desperately invested in getting her off my back and winning her approval at the same time. I hadn't learned to manage my expectations. That would come years later, after I got sober.

In my most panicked moments back then, I didn't think she loved me unconditionally. The conditions? They changed, depending on my insecurity of the month. She wanted me to be straight, girlier, prettier, smarter—a million things I felt I wasn't. But then she would do something like send me $50 just when I needed it, or make me red sauce and a German chocolate cake for dessert when I came home to visit or give me a cookbook for my birthday with an inscription that made me cry.

I don't know that she sees it this way, but I think she had not yet found the kind of mellowness that comes with living long enough to have seen almost everything, and to realize very little of it can be changed. That includes who your children turn out to be and diseases that might be hiding out in your genes.

To finally learn to love my mother and myself, I had to become an adult. And for me, one small but important part of becoming an adult was learning a recipe from start to finish, then mastering it so the dish is pitch-perfect every time.

Can you recall the first grown-up recipe you really mastered? It's likely not the first thing you ever made, the misshapen pancakes cooked at your father's elbow or a batch of cookies crammed with too many M&Ms. And it is likely not the first few experiments when you left home, the ones you made to impress a date or because it was your turn in the kitchen at the shared house you lived in during college.

That special dish usually comes once you are old enough to have someone to cook for and mature enough to understand the value in mastering a recipe so that its preparation is as routine as making a bed with fresh sheets, and the results as predictably nice.

My first was a tomato sauce recipe on page 95 of that Marcella Hazan book my mother gave me. It starts with a couple of pounds of tomatoes. Marcella always prefers the long, thick-walled Romas, and only the ones that are grown naturally and ripen in the summer. When I have those, from a little garden of my own or from a farmers' market, I use them. Otherwise, I reach for the can.

You put two pounds of chopped Romas and their juice (or two cups of their canned brethren) in a pot with a lid and set the pot to simmer for about ten minutes. Then you send the tomatoes through a food mill or, in a pinch, a food processor. Next, you stir in a stick of butter, a quarter teaspoon of sugar and a good pinch of salt. Cut a medium yellow onion in half, peel it and set it cut side down into the tomatoes. Let everything simmer as slowly as possible for about forty-five minutes. Take out the onion and see if the sauce needs more salt.

The recipe is ridiculously easy and reliably delicious. You can make it in a stranger's kitchen and instantly become a beloved guest. I toss it with whatever pasta might be around, which is usually simple spaghetti. Sometimes I rice a couple of potatoes and make gnocchi.

Marcella says it works best on gnocchi. A couple of times I spooned it over halibut that friends and I caught when I lived in Alaska. And when I had time for a project, I rolled out my own pasta.

A couple of years ago, I ended up standing in front of a bin of pale tomatoes, thinking about that recipe. I was at a Publix supermarket a short drive north of Marcella Hazan's condo. She had some years earlier moved to Longboat Key, which was little more than a stretch of floury white sand and condominiums that stood like fortresses against the Gulf of Mexico. She and her husband, Victor, decided to make Florida home after decades in glorious locations like Milan and a sixteenth-century palazzo in Venice. They wanted to be close to their only son, Giuliano.

In an hour, I would be sitting at her table for lunch, interviewing the woman whose book symbolized so much to me about cooking, about being an adult and about my mother.

Superimposed over the whole scene was my own daughter, who was a mere seven months old. It would probably be a few years until I would have time to make my own pasta again, or even mix up a batch of gnocchi. But even before she was born, I fantasized often about how I would teach her to love the kitchen, to knead pasta dough and carefully stir a pot.

When would that be? When can you have a child at your knee when hot oil and sharp knives are involved? I had no idea. At this point, neither Katia nor I had anything close to a clue about raising a child. We were barely out of the fog that rolls in with a first child, paging through parenting books like strung-out scholars.

We lived in Brooklyn, thousands of miles from either of our mothers. There were no aunties around, either. A few of our friends had children, and we clung to their every word. They were our "momtourage" and they saved us regularly. But mostly, we knew we were in over our heads. Deliriously in love with Sammy, but over our heads.

I had started cooking almost as soon as we got home from the hospital, but I couldn't manage much more than that. Thankfully, Katia had had a sweet and relatively easy delivery, but things still hurt and we were both baffled by our lovely, tiny daughter. We needed help. So we hired an Italian doula named Diana for a couple of weeks. Diana was a blessing, showing us how to slip Sammy into the sink for a bath and how to hold her in the most soothing ways. She helped Katia figure out how to breast-feed and even did some laundry and answered the phone because we couldn't form complete sentences.

My friend who referred her told us she made great fruit salad, but Diana never had the chance. In fact, I made her lunches and slipped her little snacks. I even shared some raw eggs in their shells that had been sitting in a jar with a black truffle.

"She said that she never let any other parent cook for her," Katia told me later. "But it seemed like you needed to be in the kitchen. She said there was no talking you out of it."

And I suppose that's true. The kitchen is where I learned all my lessons. It's where I go when I don't know what else to do. So there was no question that our daughter would grow up cooking. Food was already central in our house, and from the minute we got Sammy home, we ate at the table for almost every meal—even though she might only be breast-feeding.

But would Sammy want to cook? Would I teach her the Marcella sauce and cheer her on when she found her own favorite? Would I give her the cookbook my mother gave me or would I send her entirely different ones, leaving her to wrap them with her own meaning? All of this ran through my mind as I stood there in that Florida

Publix, the store where Marcella, the woman who taught America's home cooks how to make true Italian food, shopped for groceries.

I was going to lunch so I could interview Marcella and Victor, in advance of what they said would be the last book the pair would ever create: *Amarcord: Marcella Remembers.*

Before we met for lunch, I wanted to do a little research, which is what brought me to the Publix. I needed to get a sense of where one of the greatest Italian cooking teachers in my lifetime shopped for food. Musicians warm up by running through scales. Professional athletes stretch. I'm a food writer. Often, my pre-interview prep involves cooking several of my subject's dishes or eating at his restaurant or walking through the aisles of the supermarket or farmers' market she cooks from.

I was already feeling a little uncomfortable. I just never imagined that one of my kitchen heroes, one of the women who helped teach me to cook and drew me closer to my mother—a woman who, in fact, I wanted to impress in the way I wanted to impress my mother—would end up in a Florida condo, forced to shop at a grocery store with tomatoes as pale as pink carnations and hybrid artichokes as big as a baby's head.

Aside from me, a couple of people working the registers and a younger man helping his mother shop, most everyone moving through the wide aisles was well on their way to seventy or beyond. A big display of inflatable alligators and lobsters—beach toys for the grandkids—hung over the entrance, serenaded by what must be the last working Muzak tape in the country.

To shop here, Marcella had to make her way past a thousand items that one would never find in the markets of Bologna and Venice, where she used to shop and where in my fantasy she would be living out her days. There were jars of sticky-looking bruschetta topping and bags of preshredded "Italian blend" cheese. All the meat had been cut into uniform sizes and laid to rest on white foam trays. There was not a butcher in sight.

"People don't know muscles anymore," she would complain to me later that day.

Even though things were grim in the Publix, walking through even the crappiest grocery store always has a way of calming me down. People tend to be nicer when they are shopping for food than, say, clothes. There's a certain low-level tribal buzz, an unspoken acknowledgment that everyone is just trying to figure out dinner. It's hard for me to be nervous in a grocery store.

Still, I had plenty to be nervous about.

This was going to be a tough interview on several levels. At eighty-four, Marcella had not been feeling that well. A parade of Marlboro Lights and afternoon shots of Gentleman Jack whiskey had added up. She had recently endured an infected foot. She also had circulation problems and a host of other ailments that come in endless waves after a certain age. She was not, as my father would say, too sparky.

As a result, she couldn't get to the store much anymore. Her health had gotten so bad that walking a block was hard. Besides, she never learned to drive. But when she did shop, with help from her son or her husband or perhaps a dedicated friend, people still recognized her. They would call out to her, or even touch her.

She found it odd and slightly annoying.

"Why they want to know me? I don't remember them," she said. "I feel bad, but I don't know how I know them."

I was also nervous because she had a reputation as one of the crankiest cookbook authors around. Pity the journalist who shows up ill-equipped to converse in the ways of the Italian kitchen. Ask the wrong question at the wrong time, and you'd face belittlement or, worse, get frozen out completely. Victor, who often speaks for both of them, still sends barbed letters to food editors and writers, many of whom keep the notes as souvenirs.

I would not be able to bear it if they ended up hating me, too. I had spent years of my life with her books. Like all Italian women, she made me think of my mother. What if the afternoon didn't work out at all?

Well, too bad. I had a story to get. And, it turns out, a couple more lessons to learn.

Every day, no matter what was going on in their lives or in the world at large, Marcella and Victor sat down for a long lunch. They started the custom back before Marcella became famous and held on to it as if it were kidney dialysis. Visitors, book tours, personal appointments—nothing got in the way of lunch.

"We are Italian," said Victor, as if that explained it all.

Actually, Victor was born in an Italian town near Marcella's but had been raised in New York City. He comes from a family of Turkish-born Sephardic Jews (just like, I might note, my Katia, whose family immigrated to Cuba instead of Italy).

Victor met Marcella when he had gone back to Italy in his twenties to reconnect with his roots, to eat and to write. Marrying her might well have been the luckiest day of his life. Or hers. It depends on your point of view.

Marcella doesn't really cook much herself anymore. But Victor does, and for special events like our lunch they get some help. This time, it was from a woman Marcella met at a party and whom she called her last student.

To get into their condo, which is on the beach side of a towering peach-colored building, I first had to stop at a compact guard shack. The guard inside, a stern, tanned man in pressed Dockers, was used to people pulling up and asking about the Hazans. People sometimes found her phone number and called, asking to stop by to have a book signed. Victor usually made them drop it off here. Marcella, often stuck in the condo by herself, sometimes let them up.

"I am the soft heart," she said.

I made my way up the elevator, down a long hall and then knocked on their door. Victor opened it and immediately grasped my hand, pulling me inside. He had long been the more physical and dapper of the two, spry as a goat and a regular with a personal trainer. He still dressed like a ladies' man in sharp linen pants and monogrammed shirts undone enough to offer a peek at his chest.

He led me into the living room. Marcella was in a modest easy chair. I knew not to extend my right hand, because hers is undersized and bent. She broke it in a fall on a beach in Egypt when she was seven. A series of botched surgeries in Italy left it deformed but still useful enough to hold a paring knife. In her memoir, she describes it like a claw, confessing that for years she would cringe when she saw herself on television.

Before they had moved in, Victor had supervised an elaborate remodel of the apartment, whose best feature is a series of tall, wide windows with gulf views. He loves things Oriental, so he had a giant Japanese screen installed near one wall. She put her wooden spoons in a Chinese brush holder. There were touches like that all over. A big, flat-screen television was mounted high on a wall, and DVDs of Fellini and Scorsese films were lined up like soldiers on a bookshelf. The New Yorker fiction issue was next to the toilet.

The small kitchen was entirely clever. Marcella had the stove moved so she could look out across the dining room to the water. She didn't want the stove facing the wall. "When I have to stare at the wall I feel I am being punished," she said.

It had a glass hood, so as not to break up the sight lines. I looked at it and thought, You'd have to clean that every night.

But there were other sweet touches I made note of, things I might adapt if I ever have another kitchen to remodel. A rolling garbage cart allowed her to pare and peel and chop wherever she chose. Platters got stored in flat, wide drawers built under the cabinets where most of us have kickboards.

An espresso machine was on the counter. Marcella started the day with a double espresso and often ended it with long talks on the phone with friends. In the afternoon, she liked to nap in her bedroom, where she also wrote her draft of the memoir. She set out everything she could remember on a legal pad. It took six months. Then she handed it to Victor, who spent another eighteen months at the computer on his sleek glass desk in an office filled with art from their travels.

That's how it has been ever since the couple began. Her recipes and her stories began in Italian, then got translated by and interpreted through Victor. They had developed a kind of third voice, even though all of their work went out under her name.

I could tell from the preparations that making lunch for a journalist still mattered to the Hazans. After all, it was a lunch with a journalist that launched Marcella's career in 1971. *The New York Times* food editor Craig Claiborne came to their apartment on the corner of Sixth Avenue and 55th Street. He had heard that Marcella was teaching the most wonderful Italian cooking classes.

That day, Marcella had made Roman-style artichokes and tortellini stuffed with ricotta and Swiss chard. She rolled veal and braised it, and shaved raw fennel into a salad. Claiborne was excited to report that it was real Italian food. It wasn't the stuff of the daughters of immigrants, the Italian-American dishes soaked in olive oil and red sauce that my mother taught me to make.

Marcella had ended up teaching cooking classes because she found herself alone in America with nothing else to do. Victor had moved her to New York, and her main job was to keep house and make the food. Marcella was not a natural housewife. And she was not the sort of person who did well without a project. She was an intellectual woman who knew how to teach. She had earned doctorates in natural sciences and biology, and was teaching math and science at a teacher's training college south of Cesenatico, the little fishing village where she grew up, when they met.

In the book, Marcella described him as persuasive, pushy and sure of himself.

"To my dismay, he was brusquely dismissive of anyone wasting time on science when they could be spending it on literature and art," she wrote.

But Marcella was slowly enchanted. They married and she dutifully followed him back and forth across the Atlantic as he struggled between trying to help his father's fur business in New York and his own wanderlust.

When they finally settled in New York, Marcella gagged at ketchup. She thought American coffee tasted like dishwater. She stumbled badly over English. All she had to do was cook for Victor, but since she hadn't spent much time in the kitchen, it was a frustrating pursuit. She eventually turned to a cookbook written by Ada Boni, a fellow Emilia-Romagna native. That was the key.

"Cooking came to me as though it had been there all along,

waiting to be expressed; it came as words come to a child when it is time for her to speak," she wrote.

In 1969, she signed up for a Chinese cooking class with Grace Chu, who canceled after one session. Her classmates decided they wanted to learn Italian cooking with Marcella instead. Victor, sensing an opportunity, encouraged it. "He said, 'You like to teach, you like to cook,'" Marcella recalled. "'Put the two things together and stop complaining.'"

With sudden fame, they went on to open cooking schools in Bologna, Venice and New York. Victor organized the classes and field trips, acting as much as tour guide as producer. He became a wine expert in his own right and published two books.

All through their relationship, they fought. Their arguments have sometimes been big and public. But this late in the relationship, they were sweet with each other even when they didn't agree. Always, Victor knew Marcella was the talent. By the time I met them, he was still talking about her like she was Muhammad Ali in his prime. As we sat down to lunch, I asked if she really deserved her reputation as a stern and sometimes downright mean teacher. He was dismissive.

The problem, he explained, was ill-behaved students who asked silly questions.

"Marcella is very tightly focused," he said. "She finds people's questions distracting."

Marcella jumped in.

"What can I do?" she said. "If you are frying something and just in a second or two you have to turn it and someone says, 'When you cut your meat, why do you hold your knife in that way?' I'm sorry. I can't tell you."

Before we moved from the living room to the dining table near the kitchen to start lunch, Victor had set out a little snack. He had instructed their cooking student to thinly slice some tuna bottarga, a cured, pressed roe that is very rich and salty, and tuck it between small squares of buttered pane carasau, or sheet music bread. Victor explained how the Sardinians roll out large, thin sheets of dough, bake them until they puff, and then separate the halves and bake them again. Although a lot of people think the name has to do with the paper-thinness and the shape of the cracker, Victor told me the music reference is because of the sound the crispy bread makes when it is set to cool on the beds of the Sardinian cooks.

He served it with flutes of Prosecco, which I just pushed to the side and hoped he didn't take note of. I watched Marcella, who wasn't having any, either. She had stopped drinking wine, Victor explained, after a hernia made her stomach too acidic. Wine had started to taste like vinegar. I didn't have a hernia for an excuse, but I hadn't had a drink in ten years by this point. I figured out a long time ago that I didn't need to explain it to anyone. Or, if I did, I usually made a joke about how they really didn't want to see me drunk.

But still, in rare circumstances, my alcoholism still makes me feel weird and out of place. And this was one of the days. I was sure I would get some kind of lecture from Victor about it. And I didn't want Marcella to think less of me, to think I was weak or not a true culinarian. I really did want her to like me in a way I don't usually feel about interview subjects. This was Marcella Hazan, whose book my mother chose to give me when I was just starting my life after college. It didn't really matter, as I began to think about a lifetime of my mother's cooking, that I realized she never really cooked Marcella's food that much. She'd get on a little jag with something like a risotto or a new way to roast pork, but she'd soon fall back on the Italian food she knew, what she grew up with. Especially as she got older. Those flavors from her childhood became more important.

That's the thing about Italian food. It's so personal. And for me, someone without a hometown and parents from very different cultures, Italian food—my mother's food—became an emotional touchstone.

So yeah, I wanted my mother's—uh, I mean Marcella's—approval, plain and simple.

For lunch, Marcella had the woman who was helping her cook pare down monster hybrid artichokes from the Publix and set pieces of the extra-large hearts in a sauté pan to brown well. The method coaxes out some flavor. Then the student layered the pieces into a baking dish with shrimp and slices of fresh mozzarella and moistened the whole casserole with olive oil and butter.

It was a delicious and unusual combination, knocking out conventional Italian notions about mixing cheese and seafood. Marcella and Victor first tasted the juicy dish in Rome. She re-created it and handed her detailed notes—in Italian, of course—to him. He translated them into a workable English-language recipe and added an elegant little headnote. The result was published a decade ago in *Marcella Cucina*, the fifth of her six cookbooks.

After lunch, over her whiskey and my espresso and a slice of semifreddo, I relaxed a little and talked some about my wife, Katia, and our new baby.

"You will bring beautiful Samantha," Marcella said, extending an invitation I doubted I would ever accept.

Then Victor played a funny recording from Danny Kaye, the

actor who became an obsessive home chef. In it, he pretends to be Marcella's Italian assistant when a woman calls Marcella's house looking for advice. We laughed, then we started talking about their son, and I talked about my mother.

Here was my moment. Through my own talents and ambition, I had made it to Marcella's kitchen. I had drawn the line from my mother's gift—the book that came when we had just begun to know each other—and the woman who wrote it. It would be magical. Maybe I would finally fill in a little more of the part of me that started in the kitchen and ended with a longing for my mother's unconditional love.

"My mother taught me to cook," I said.

"Of course," she said.

"The first real cookbook she ever gave me is *The Classic Italian Cook Book*," I said.

"It is a good book, that one. Why she didn't give you more?"

"I . . . well," I start to stammer.

Then Victor hands her the bottle of Gentleman Jack. She nestles it in her bad arm and screws off the lid, pouring a good two fingers over half-moons of ice from the icemaker. Marcella was starting to look bored. There would be no magic moment, nothing to take back and share with my mother. There would be no revelation.

Not that I knew what I was looking for, really. I wasn't sure, at that moment, how much my mother really cared about Marcella. I knew I had placed Marcella on some kind of cloud, that she was a surrogate of sorts. Or maybe a spiritual link to my ailing mother.

But really, Marcella was just Marcella. She is a great Italian cook whose book fell into my hands, who is as flawed as any of us.

In the end, I would never get Marcella's approval. My problem was that I had attached too much to the outcome of our meeting. That's a game you'll never win.

Still, I wasn't going down without a fight. And all I had left was a party trick. I told Marcella how much Rachael Ray admired her.

"Well," said Marcella in her Italian-tinged English. "I likka her, too. She does a real good job."

"So," I said, "why don't you tell her yourself?"

I whipped out my cell phone and dialed Rachael's number.

I went back to New York and wrote a story for the *Times*. I thought it was a loving but clear-eyed assessment of them. Fair, not fawning, and with information about the couple no one had ever read. My editors loved it, and so did plenty of readers.

But whether cigarettes and whiskey affected Marcella's ability to taste food became a big point of contention in the story. Before I had traveled to Florida, I'd had lunch in a fancy restaurant near Central Park with Judith Jones, once Marcella's editor.

"Marcella has long ago burned out her palate on bourbon and cigarettes," she told me during lunch. In her own memoir, Judith wrote about the difficult relationship she had with the Hazans, and about how particular and stubborn the couple could be. They answered her accusations in their book, calling Judith unqualified to judge Marcella's work and a poor cook. At the end of their relationship, Marcella was crying in a restaurant, begging to be let out of her contract because Judith and the publisher treated one of her books, *Essentials of Classic Italian Cooking*, so poorly.

Marcella will argue that cigarettes have improved her palate to the point where even the slightest off flavors in food make her sick. I pointed all of this out in a short passage in the story, which I thought presented it and the rest of their lives in a way that was fair and without judgment.

Victor didn't see it that way. He fired off some of the angriest e-mails I have ever received. As a food writer, I don't get a lot of hate mail, but there are always notes from a self-righteous animal rights activist, the diva unaccustomed to getting poked or other assorted readers who just get mad about how I approach a pet topic.

These, though, topped them all. Because I had so much tied up in Marcella and my mother, it was like getting a nasty letter from a member of the family.

"I regret that you chose to print Judith's shrewish remark about Marcella's damaged palate," he wrote. "You should have been in an excellent position to rebut it, having recently tasted the product of that palate."

He went on.

"The statement was allowed to drop there unchallenged, creating a false image of Marcella as a nicotine fiend and a lush. It was a low blow."

He suggested I was perhaps better suited for the *National Enquirer*.

Then he dealt the most painful punch.

"Imagine how Marcella felt."

Every guilt-soaked bone in my body ached. But only for a second. I was getting pretty good at recognizing emotional manipulation. And it soon became clear he wanted to simply inflict pain but not destroy me. I was still useful to him. At the end of one of his meanest e-mails, he made sure to invite me to their book party in New York.

I didn't go, but I realized that meeting Marcella had helped me finally untangle a few things. I had such high expectations for the visit, such high hopes that in addition to a story I would get some kind of resolution, some kind of approval, and I would get closer to my mom.

What I got was an understanding that I am always a victim of my own expectations. And if I have expectations, it means I am trying to control a situation. And that means I am always going to be disappointed. Because you can't control people.

But that would not be the only thing I had to learn. I still had to find one final piece of resolution with my mother.

Around the time I met Marcella, my mother became very sick with one of those hospital-grade infections.

Despite the Parkinson's, she kept hosting bridge parties and sending out birthday presents and bowling, her shaky arm some-how still able to send the ball down the lane with enough frequency that she would occasionally win the pot of money collected from all the bowlers, each one hoping they would have the highest score or complete the most spares.

She even golfed a little, and she volunteered at the town hospi-tal. "You have to help the old people," she told me. But the time when all that ends and she will need a lot of help is getting closer. Each time I see her, I worry it will be the last time I see her walk.

In order to keep comfortable and active as long as possible, my mother had decided to have her knee replaced. I had been out to visit when she had the surgery, and things had gone fine. But a few weeks afterward, my father called. There had been a complication. Somehow, she'd contracted a horrible staph infection. They had to take out the new knee and replace it with another one. She would have to have an IV feeding antibiotics into her body twenty-four

hours a day for at least six weeks. If they couldn't control the infection, she might have to get her leg amputated above the knee.

I flew out as soon as I could, staying on until she was out of the
hospital. But we were still very deep in the woods. The infection had
to be flushed and the new knee had to take. The odds were good,
but not great. They sent her home with a machine to keep her knee
in motion when she was in bed and a blue fanny pack that held
medicine that had to be replenished daily. A clear, thin tube sent
the medicine from the pack into her arm. The clear fluid in that
little tube became sacred. We all hoped that it would save her life.
We had to believe it.

I spent the first few days helping her with basic things. Although
my mother never met a good cry she didn't like, she has always been
self-sufficient and physically private. As a kid, I never saw her naked.
I can barely recall that she was sick. But now she needed help getting
her clothes on and off, and getting to the bathroom. I was happy to
do it, but the intimacy of it all made us both uncomfortable.

She was so weak she could barely lift her arms above her head
and the big incision in her knee meant she couldn't take a shower.
So I helped her move slowly into the bathroom so she could wash
up a little.

I rummaged around in the bathroom cabinets looking for a
washcloth and anything else I might need for the sponge bath. I
found some old Epsom salts and put them in a plastic tub so she
could soak her feet. Then I dug up some hospital-grade body wash,
a relic from when her mother-in-law—my father's mother—died. This
was a woman who almost didn't go to my parents' wedding because
her perfect Norwegian son was marrying an Italian girl from a farm.
Her feelings mellowed through the years, and she came to be the

kind of grandmother who remembered you with a $5 bill on your birthdays and pajamas at Christmas.

My mother nursed that woman until she died.

I put some of the soap on a washcloth and dunked it in warm water. My mother's hand was on my shoulder, shaking only barely. I helped her wash.

Over the next week, she started to feel much better. And we began to have longer talks, over coffee at her kitchen table. One of them was about Marcella Hazan. I told my mother I wanted to write about Marcella in part because of the cookbook she had given me twenty-five years earlier. She remembered the book, but she didn't remember why she gave me that one in particular.

"I guess I just liked it and I thought you would," she said. "You always liked cookbooks."

Again, it's those expectations. For my mom, it was a nice book she thought I'd like. For me it was some kind of talisman, connecting me to a culture and my mother. My connection to the kitchen—and to the great women cooks I would later become so enchanted with—was all about finding a connection to my mother.

I kept pushing. Did she think I was a good cook, even back then? Was I always interested in cooking? What kind of child was I? The questions poured out. I was hungry for answers. I didn't get many.

"Well, you were in the kitchen with me a lot," she said.

Although I am not sure what I really wanted to hear, her answers were wholly unsatisfying. I moved into deeper territory. Did she remember the letter I wrote to her about being gay, back when I was just getting out of college? She didn't, but then she told me how much she loves Katia and how excited she is about her newest granddaughter.

Did she ever wish we had talked more, talked earlier?

"I suppose," she said, "but what's done is done."

And that's really it. What's done is done. It's kind of a mantra for my mother. For her, the phrase signals that it's time to stop wallowing and move on. You can't change the past. What is, is and what's done is done.

I never used to understand those expressions. But now I see them as more useful than any other tool she could have given me. They signal acceptance, and acceptance is the key to my happiness.

Of all the lessons I have learned from the wise women of the kitchen—that I can always start over, to be true to myself, to stop measuring myself against other people, to have faith and humility and to always stay close to family—it came down to this. The past is past and I have no control over the future. Letting go of all the pain and missteps in my past and embracing hope in tomorrow is the only way I will be truly happy today.

I work every day on being grateful for what I have, even if it is not what I planned.

I accept what comes my way.

What other choice is there?

The doorbell interrupted our talk. It was the UPS driver with a box of peaches from Nell Newman.

When I worked for the *San Francisco Chronicle*, I had written a profile on Nell Newman, the daughter of Paul Newman and Joanne Woodward. She's the one who convinced her father to start an organic line of his Newman's Own food company.

Nell lived in a sweet little house in Northern California. A prolific Babcock peach tree in the backyard was her obsession. She canceled travel plans when the peaches were ripe so she could be around to harvest them. If she had to leave the house, she would sometimes put air mattresses underneath the tree so the fruit that fell wouldn't bruise. Over the years, we kept in touch. She would talk to me about the organic food business, and she once arranged things so I could interview her parents over dinner when her father helped open a restaurant in Westport, Connecticut.

Just after I landed in Colorado, she had called me, looking for a reporter who might investigate an insurance nightmare one of her employees was facing. I gave her a couple of names.

"I have to go," I said. "I'm at my mom's house. She's sick."

She asked what was going on, so I told her the short version of the story.

"Give me your mom's address," she said.

The UPS driver was holding a box with three perfect Babcock whites.

"These are peaches from Paul Newman's daughter?" my mother asked. "Paul Newman, the actor?"

At first, Carnival Daughter kicked in. I wanted to show off for her. I wanted her to see me. For a brief second I was the child running home with a trophy from the softball tournament, cooking dinner for my family and praying for another badge to sew onto my Girl Scout sash.

But the feeling lasted only a moment. I smiled. I knew the peaches would make her happy and, if only for an afternoon, distract her from her pain and worry. It was, at that moment, more important for me to care for her than to have her care for me. I was no longer a child.

The first two I peeled and sliced and put over good vanilla ice cream for dessert. I handed one bowl to my mom and one to my dad, who probably needed the distraction more than any of us. By the end of the next day, the last peach was so ripe I decided we had to eat it immediately.

I walked over to the sink and rinsed it off. My mom set her walker aside and joined me. We leaned over the sink and I took a bite. It was pure peach, pure sun. I handed it over, and watched the juice run onto her chin. We worked our way back and forth like that until we got to the pit, which I held so she could get the last bite.

"That was good," she said, reaching for her walker. "Make sure you tell Nell."

She eased her way back to the den. I cleaned up and followed her. She had settled down on the couch and was watching *Little House on the Prairie.*

The night before I left, she fell asleep in the living room. It was still early in the evening. She couldn't even stay up to watch her Colorado Rockies beat the Milwaukee Brewers. My dad was always a baseball fan, but not so much my mother. But now, late in her life, she was crazy for it. I can't figure out if she really loves the game or if she decided to get into baseball as a way to share something with my father. They've been married for well over fifty years. She's probably onto something.

I cuddled next to her and adjusted the towel that we wrapped around the place where the IV needle goes into her arm. It's hooked up to an alarm that beeps if the flow of medicine stops.

My mother opened her eyes.

"I love you," she said. "You are such a good daughter."

"I love you, too," I said. "You are such a good mother."

She reached up to hug me and her IV started to beep. I adjusted it. She was shaky, so I helped her sit up and move her leg so she would be comfortable.

"Oh Kimmie, it's too early for you to have to take care of me."

"No, it's not, Mom," I said. "No, it's not."

And I headed into the kitchen to make her something good to eat.

Acknowledgments

Thank you, first, to the Seversons: my parents, Anne and Jim, and my siblings, Keith, Kent, Keely and Kris. I love you all so much.

Next up, a very special thanks to my wife, Katia Hetter. You took care of my head and my heart and all the family business while I was hunched over a laptop at the dining room table.

A big thank-you (is that hyphenated?) to all the editors who have ever had to wrestle with my copy. The list starts with Bob Button, former advisor to the staff of *The Tower* at Grosse Point South High School, and ends with my current crew of magic hands at *The New York Times*. (A few hold a special place, and you know who you are Jan Brandt, Kathleen McCoy, Howard Weaver, Michael Bauer and Miriam Morgan.)

As for the matter at hand, give it up for the smooth Sarahs, along with the rest of the Riverhead team behind this book. Sarah McGrath is exactly the editor I needed, a perfect mix of smarts, compassion and wisdom. Sarah Stein had her capable hand on the rudder to the very end.

Thanks to my agent, Heather Schroeder, for pulling this book out of me.

I had readers, many great readers. Thom Geier is at the top of the heap. Thanks for believing there was a book in that pile of paper I handed you.

To Bennett Brooks, Kent Severson, Cindy Burke, Jill Agostino, Carolyn Ryan and Julia Moskin: Thank you for the smart reads and for always having my back.

Thanks to Jessica DuLong, Frank Bruni, Pableaux Johnson, Sarah Rohen and all the other authors who told me over and over that the agony I felt writing this book was perfectly normal.

Thanks to Holly Leicht, Heather O'Donnell, Julie Friesen and Leanh Nguyen for giving me space to write when I really needed it.

Thanks to Scott Peacock and the other people who introduced me to the women who are profiled in this book.

Thanks, Bill.

And my deepest gratitude to the women themselves. They are true heroes of the kitchen.

Kim Severson has been a food writer for *The New York Times* since 2004. Previously, she was a food writer and editor at the *San Francisco Chronicle*, where she won national awards for news and feature writing, including the Casey Medal for Meritorious Journalism, and four James Beard Foundation awards for food writing. She has been a newspaper journalist since high school, a career that has taken her to six states. In addition to food, she has covered crime, education, social services, and government. Born in Wisconsin and raised in Texas and Michigan, she now lives in Brooklyn with her partner, Katia Hetter, and their daughter.